P<

MW01156926

Richard Benedetto

University Press of America,® Inc.

Copyright © 2006 by
University Press of America,® Inc.
4501 Forbes Boulevard
Suite 200
Lanham, Maryland 20706
UPA Acquisitions Department (301) 459-3366

PO Box 317
Oxford
OX2 9RU, UK

Library of Congress Control Number: 2006900092
ISBN-13: 978-0-7618-3422-9 (paperback : alk. paper)
ISBN-10: 0-7618-3422-2 (paperback : alk. paper)

♾™ The paper used in this publication meets the minimum
requirements of American National Standard for Information
Sciences—Permanence of Paper for Printed Library Materials
ANSI Z39.48—1984

To
Carol

Contents

vi

Foreword

Hail To Candor,
Curiosity, Civility

This is a memoir with twist. What began as a look back over 35 years of reporting by a renowned journalist evolved into a celebration of politics and the politicians he covered. Unlike many commentators today, Richard Benedetto lets his reportage do the talking. His tactic for this book: Find what's right with politics and the politicians who practice it.

From the grassroots of local government and backrooms of city halls to the manicured lawns and Oval Office of 1600 Pennsylvania Avenue, Benedetto has interviewed presidents, governors, mayors, village council members and clerks in municipal offices. He has covered 16 national conventions since 1976 and landed assignments in every state in the USA and more than a dozen countries.

For all of his civility and sunny nature, Benedetto is no stranger to aggressive reporting. His investigations into questionable city and state financial practices have won needed reforms and gained major journalism awards. His detailed examination of declassified documents shed new light on the 1961 Bay of Pigs invasion of Cuba. Early in his career, an exposé on the performance of street-cleaning crews was pivotal in a mayoral election.

I have known and worked with Richard Benedetto since 1978, first at *Gannett News Service*, then for 20-plus years at USA TODAY. I served there as national editor, managing editor of News and from 1995-2002, executive editor of the newspaper. He is impartial, tireless and insatiably curious—always making one more phone call for a quote, mingling with crowds on the campaign trail for one more anecdote and pressing hard to "get the other side" into controversial stories. His reputation for integrity, fairness, courage and character is second to none.

Benedetto's byline graced the front-page cover story of the first edition of USA TODAY on September 15, 1982. Because the newspaper's aggressive use of color, snapshots and informational graphics changed the face of print journalism across the USA, a colorful snapshot of politicians by one of the paper's most prolific reporters is fitting.

Reporters are people, too.

Robert Dubill
Alexandria, Va.
February 2006

viii

Preface

This book is about promises.

Promises to my grandmother and mother, who said I should always try to find the good in people.

A promise to my grandfather, who said to work hard at whatever I do, be respectful to politicians, be proud of my Italian heritage and be thankful to be an American.

A promise to my friend and mentor, the late Ralph Soda, who made me promise him that I would write this book.

And a promise to myself to never forget where I came from.

Richard Benedetto
Washington, D.C.
February 2006

x

Acknowledgements

My sincere thanks to my agent, Donna Luh, who sparked the start of this book and pushed it to completion.

My deep gratitude to three top-notch editors and friends, Bob Dubill, Frank Tomaino and Tony Vella, who not only taught me, guided me and inspired me throughout my career, but also generously helped edit this manuscript and make valuable suggestions for improvements. As newsmen and as friends, they are the best.

To every politician I covered, my admiration for your service and my thanks for the memories, which I will always cherish.

Chapter One

"You Don't Boo the President of the United States"

I have been a government and political newspaper reporter for more than three decades, and I still believe that politicians are people, too. By the time I was 10 years old, my grandfather had already taught me to treat politicians with respect. And some very wise editors I worked for early in my career advised me to treat the people I was writing about fairly and with dignity, no matter how small their accomplishments or how big their errors. Those lessons never left me and served as a guide not only for my career, but also for this book.

I start with my grandfather, an Italian immigrant whose name was Cosmo, a man of the stars. He was a proud American with a deep and sincere love for his adopted country. As a young man, in America only a few years, he enlisted in the United States Army during World War I and fought with the 68th Lightning Division in the Argonne Forest in France, where he was awarded the Purple Heart after inhaling poison gas sprayed on the battlefield by the Germans. He was a victim of chemical weapons. While my grandfather was convalescing from his gassing at a Veteran's Hospital in Perryville, Md., he became a U.S. citizen, a day he recalled many years later as one of the indelible high points of his life.

"I became an American citizen in Baltimore, Md.," he would say, never forgetting to mention the name of the state as well as the city, as if people might not be sure what state Baltimore was in. He also pronounced it "Mary-Land," probably as it was at the time of its charter as an English colony in 1635, when the Mid-Atlantic state was named after Queen Henrietta Maria, wife of King George I.

My grandfather and I were very close as I was growing up in Utica, a small industrial city on the Mohawk River in Central New York. Its cotton mills - world-famous Utica Sheets were once made there - and railroad yards were magnets for many poor Italian-American immigrants who came to America looking for work and a place to raise their children, who they believed could be anything they wanted to be. During World

2 *"You Don't Boo the President of the United States"*

War II, when my farther was in the Marine Corps fighting the Japanese in the South Pacific, my grandfather was the main man in my life in my pre-school years. We lived in the same two-family house and wherever he went, I adoringly followed, like a shadow. He was a florist and he would take me along in his maroon 1940 Chevrolet truck, a sedan delivery which was a lot like today's Chrysler PT Cruiser. With good coaching from my grandfather, by age five I could name the brand of most cars on the road, and in many cases, their model years, as well. He kept me sharp by quizzing me as the cars rolled past. I loved my grandfather's truck, which he kept clean and shiny. He didn't want his customers to think they were dealing with a second-rate florist. The truck had "Paradise Flower Shop" written in fancy script on the side, and when we rolled down the street I felt like I was riding in a limousine. We would deliver bouquets and baskets to hospitals and funeral homes, haul large cardboard boxes of gladiolas shipped by Railway Express from Florida or pick up massive cakes of ice from the ice house for the huge, glass-doored flower coolers in his shop. Knowing that I was familiar with the routes to these places, having been there with him so many times, he developed a little game. He would say he forgot how to get there and ask me the directions. So as we went, I would tell him where to turn right and where to turn left, proud of myself thinking that were it not for me, we would have gotten lost and these vital pickups and deliveries would never be made. I recall him saying just that to my grandmother when we returned. I would stand there and beam as she heaped praise on me for saving the day.

My grandfather also taught me to play checkers. Then, when I had learned the game sufficiently to play respectably, he would let me win, pretending to make a mistake that would lead to giving me double jumps. I remember how he would always throw his head back, clasp his hand to his forehead and wince when I would eagerly execute my jumps with an emphatic click of the checker on the board as it touched down on the other side of his hapless black disc. I always had to have the reds.

Like I said, my grandfather taught me to have respect for politicians. One Saturday afternoon back in 1951, when I was 10 years old, I was returning home from the matinee at the neighborhood movie house, the Rialto, a major center in the cultural life of our largely Italian-American neighborhood on the east side of Utica. I stopped at my grandfather's flower shop to excitedly report on the cowboy movies I saw. It was getting dark, past 5 p.m. and he was ready to close. But before he did, he was stealing a quick read of the afternoon newspaper, the *Observer-Dispatch,* which had been delivered shortly before. So clear is my recollection of that pivotal moment that I remember him leaning over, his elbows resting on the waist-high bench he arranged flowers on, the open newspaper laying flat on its smooth surface. But before I got to offering a summary of the movies, I had a burning question to ask. I was puzzled by the spontaneous, scattered booing that broke out in the movie audience when the newsreel flashed the image of President Harry Truman. At 10 years old, I knew nothing about politics. I knew that Truman was the president and that the presidency was a very important office, and that's about all. So I asked my grandfather why people booed President Truman. He stiffened, as if I had slapped him in the face, pulled himself to his full height and turned to face me. He jerked his right arm straight out and menacingly pointed his index finger toward my nose.

"You didn't boo, did you?" he asked in a loud angry voice I only heard him use maybe once or twice before.

Shocked and a little frightened, I took one step back and timidly answered, "N-n-n-no."

"Good!" he replied, still thrusting that finger toward me. "You Don't Boo The President of the United States!" He said it slowly, emphasizing each word with a downward stroke of his arm, as if he was driving a large nail into a hard piece of wood.

At the time, I took him literally. You don't boo the president of the United States. It's against the rules. Period. And I didn't. But over time, I realized that what he was really saying was that as a citizen you should have respect for the office of the presidency, or any other high elective office, even if you don't like the job the occupant is doing. More than 50 years ago, he was instructing me that there is a certain level of dignity and restraint you should use when being critical. Civility at all times. Anything less, he was telling me, was demeaning to our system. He was right. And I have tried my best to live up to those principles over my long career. As a reporter, you can disagree without being rude. You can be critical, without being discourteous. You can be tough, without being boorish. You can point out wrongdoing, without being snide or nasty and without seeming to revel in the fate that might befall a politician in trouble. The problem in today's rough-and-tumble, 24-hour media age, is that reporters seem to take pleasure in bringing the mighty down, forgetting that the American press was given so much freedom because the founders saw wide-ranging latitude to probe and criticize as a way to improve the system, not destroy it. To some cynical reporters, tearing it down seems to be the goal. Make it better? They say let somebody else worry about it. And besides, many are convinced that it will never get better anyway. So they feel free to bash away without concern for the consequences. At the core, we have a citizenry that looks to the media for cues and winds up with little confidence in or respect for their government and its leaders. Such coverage of politics is why so many people, when asked to discuss politics or politicians, scoff at the notion and say, "Forget it! They're all a bunch of bums or crooks." Who is there to tell them otherwise - that there are good politicians as well as bad ones? Sadly, we only learn of the good ones when they die and people say nice things about them. In life, the good they do is often ignored by the media. But let them foul up and it's front-page news. These days, the political water is so brackish that if someone in the media tries to set it all straight, or provide some needed balance, he or she is often accused of being soft, bought off by one side or the other, or worse, seen as journalist who is tired and has lost the way.

But I was lucky. Early in my career, I was touched by editors from an earlier generation who had different values about the news business and what it was that we were supposed to do with the great public trust that had been thrust into our hands. These editors, most from working-class backgrounds, had a feel for real people and a true empathy for the human condition - knowing full well that human beings have the capability of doing great good and making huge mistakes, often doing both at the same time. But these editors never took it upon themselves to sit in judgment and condemn. They urged the people working for them to go out and report and come back and tell what they found out. After all, in its simplest form or basic definition, news reporting is going to places where most people do not go and coming back and telling these who weren't there what you heard and saw. What could be simpler?

Therefore, under that definition, if you heard and saw something good, you reported it. And if you heard and saw something bad, you reported that. And editors were just as happy with the good as with the bad.

Today, for the most part, if something good happens when a reporter goes out and reports, it's minor news, or not news at all. But if it's bad, it's a big story. Given that incentive, is there any doubt why we seem to get a plethora of bad news and just a smidgen of good?

Moreover, we have a tendency to frame everything in terms of conflict, giving greater amplification to those who take the most extreme views and giving short shrift or ignoring those taking the most reasonable and reasoned stands. It's sexier to portray everything as a huge and nasty fight whether the issue be Social Security overhaul or abortion.

The cumulative effect of a huge imbalance between good news and bad, reasoned discussion and sharp debate, is to give the citizenry an inaccurate or distorted picture of the world around them. One key reason why many Americans believe their governments don't work, problems are intractable and their politicians are all bums, is because we overreport on the things and people that don't work and pay little attention to those that do. We need more balance in reporting and more-reasoned discussion of controversial issues. People would welcome it.

But when I was in my first journalism job back in the late 1960s, the news business was quite different. At least it was where I went to work at the *Buffalo (N.Y.) Evening News,* now the *Buffalo News.* In those days, *The News* prided itself on being the paper of record in Western New York. It covered and reported on everything from town and zoning board meetings in Gowanda to neighborhood picnics held at Crystal Beach. If the Lackawanna City Council voted to put a traffic light on a certain corner or the Batavia planning board approved an application to build a gas station on a parcel of land in the village, *The News* reported it. No one said let's not do it because it's boring or no one cares. At that time, the standard was, if it happened, people should know it. That's it. No debate. No instructions to pump or hype it up to make it sound exciting. Just report it straight, no frills, no hoopla, no running out to find somebody who was against it and give them the headline. And boring as it might have been, people in those communities read that stuff. How did we know? Make a mistake or miss a name or action and the phone would ring off the wall, causing no small amount of grief for the reporter assigned to the story. Not only did he have to explain himself to the angry reader, he had to convince a stern editor that he wasn't a fool.

One such editor was Bud Wacker, the balding city editor of *The News* who would gruffly instruct procrastinating reporters to practice what he called "cheek-to-chair" journalism: Shut up, sit down and write! One of

6 *"You Don't Boo the President of the United States"*

the first assignments Wacker sent me on was to go to Crystal Beach, a now-defunct Canadian amusement park on Lake Erie, just across the Niagara River from downtown Buffalo. Every summer, various Buffalo city neighborhood organizations would sponsor bus trips for the kids to picnic at the amusement park, scramble for the rides and compete for minor prizes in various contests such as egg rolling, beanbag throwing and sack racing. My job was to get the names of the winners in each contest, find a pay phone - no cell phones in those days - and call them in to a rewrite reporter back in the office who would type them for publication in that afternoon's paper. By the time those kids got home, they could pick up the newspaper on their doorstep and read their names under the headline - "Genesee-Moselle Neighbors (or Kenmore Neighbors or South Park Neighbors or East Aurora Neighbors or Delevan Neighbors) Have Fun at Crystal Beach."

For a rookie reporter who thought that he would be immediately assigned to covering the big murder cases or the hottest political race in town, being sent to cover eight-year-olds running in three-legged races was a good lesson in how important the people you cover are, no matter how small you may think they are. As Wacker said, most people only get their names in the paper when they are born and when they die. So for those rare in-between times when they might be mentioned, it's a big deal to them and to their families and friends, no matter how trivial it might seem to you. Therefore, he warned, you had better spell their names right, get their correct ages and their home addresses and phone numbers in case we have to double check. Starting out that way was a valuable lesson in the importance of every person whose name you put in the paper.

But it wasn't until a few years later, when I was working at the *Utica (N.Y.) Observer-Dispatch,* when that lesson was taken beyond the mere importance of every name you put into the paper to the awesome responsibility to treat that person whose name has been entrusted to you fairly. As Tony Vella, my managing editor in Utica put it in the casual, soft-but-emphatic way he had of imparting wisdom, "Remember one thing: Every name you type into your story has a real, live person attached to it." It was a simple, but startling concept. Of course those names are attached to real people. But often, in our eagerness to get the story into the paper, we see those names as just words, and fail to consider how those persons and their families will react to what we say about them, especially if we are connecting them to wrongdoing, or holding them up for ridicule for mistakes they made. Vella was not saying that I should go easy on them. He was saying that if I was going to be reporting something negative about a person, I had better be sure that first, it needs saying, second, it is correct and third, that the person has been offered a chance to defend himself or herself. That's all.

I guess I have been a reporter ever since my grandmother used to ask me to tell her about the cowboy, G-man and jungle movies I used to see on Saturday afternoons at the Rialto, the neighborhood theater known to all who lived on the predominantly Italian-American east side of Utica as "The Ri." To kids, attending the Saturday matinee at the Ri - three movies, a serial, a cartoon and the newsreel - was almost as mandatory as Sunday Mass. And every Tuesday night, women used to religiously go to the Ri to collect the free dish given to every paying customer. One night it would be soup bowls, another it would be coffee cups. Eventually, they would create a full set and give them to their daughters who were about to get married. So to make the collection of the set faster, relatives and neighbors were recruited to join the bride's mother at the Ri on Tuesday nights, a pilgrimage that came to be known as "Making the Dish." Many an East Utica newlywed couple ate in style off of flower-patterned dishware collected at the Ri, my wife Carol and I included. But only on Sundays. After all, this was the good china, not the stuff you bought at Woolworth's.

My grandmother was my first inspiration to become a reporter. She so enjoyed the way I came home and described the movies I saw that she said I should be a writer. She also instilled a love of books in me by buying a popular set of encyclopedias for children, "The Book of Knowledge." Those thick, red-bound books, 10 volumes in all, were my first windows on a world of wonder that existed beyond Utica - a world I grew curious to explore by looking at the pictures of such exotic places as Egypt and Brazil, Antarctica and India. One of the most memorable pictures was a full-page portrait of the Empire State Building, soaring to the heavens in all its streamlined glory. To me, it was the living symbol of a big, exciting world waiting for me to discover. I would return to that picture over and over to assure myself that it was real and there for me to see one day. But most of all, I liked the exciting stories those books contained - "The Legend of Sleepy Hollow," "King Arthur and his Knights of the Round Table" - and romantic poems such as "The Highwayman" and "In Flanders Field." My favorite was Charles Dickens' "A Christmas Carol," which I would repeatedly ask my grandmother to read to me year-round. I remember her remarking to mother, "He wants to hear Scrooge and it's July." But even in the sweltering heat she would patiently sit down and read about Marley's ghost and its clanking chains, a bewildered Scrooge in nightshirt, cap and slippers sitting in the shadowy candlelight.

While my grandmother planted the seed that I should be a writer, my first inspiration for my interest in politics came from my Proctor High School social studies teacher, Ann Alberico Duggan, who during my senior year assigned members of her class in Problems of Democracy to attend a Utica City Council meeting as part of her lesson on local government. I went to the next Tuesday night meeting and heard a long, spirited debate between two members of the Council over whether to put a stop light or a stop sign on a certain street corner. The contentious discussion went on so long that they adjourned the meeting to the following week. I was so fascinated by what I had seen and heard that I returned the following week on my own to hear how it came out. Mrs. Duggan was really impressed that I went back without being assigned and embarrassed me by announcing it to the class - holding me up as a model they should emulate. I just about died, and for a long time got razzed for being Mrs. Duggan's "pet." Incidentally, the street light did get approved.

One more thing about Mrs. Duggan: She often would say to the kids in her class, "Open your eyes! The world isn't bounded by Culver Ave., the Parkway, Mohawk Street and Broad Street." (The rough boundaries of East Utica , where most of her Italian-American students lived.) Many kids took that as a put-down of Italian-Americans. But she was one herself, the daughter of Italian immigrants who became successful wholesale grocers. Her advice was not meant to be derogatory. She was urging us to realize that there was a whole big world beyond the insular borders of our neighborhood and we should get out and experience it.

Mrs. Duggan had no children of her own. She never drove a car, taking the city bus to work every day. Often, while leaving baseball or football practice, I would see her waiting for the bus in front of the school, several hours after most of her colleagues had gone home for the day. She once wrote me a letter telling me how proud she was of my accomplishments, and never failed to inquire about me whenever she would run into my mother. Mrs. Duggan died in 2002, well into her 90s. Her obituary said she remained active right up to her death, mentoring young women and volunteering in various civic groups and charitable organizations. I was not surprised.

10

Chapter Two
"I Was Good, Wasn't I?"

My first taste of covering national politics came in Buffalo in 1968, a tumultuous year. It began when the surprising early success of the Viet Cong's TET offensive turned many Americans against the Vietnam War and caused Lyndon Johnson to choose not to seek re-election. After that, all hell seemed to break loose. Martin Luther King Jr. and Robert Kennedy were assassinated, racial riots tore our cities apart, college campus were hotbeds of war protest, the Democratic National Convention in Chicago was marred by violence in the streets and George Wallace, the pugnacious governor of Alabama, ran an independent campaign for president. In October, the once-segregationist Wallace brought his "Stand Up For America" road show, throbbing to the beat of country music, to Buffalo. I was one of the reporters assigned to help cover it.

More than 8,000 mostly blue-collar Wallace supporters packed the Memorial Auditorium, affectionately known in those days as "The Aud" to Western New York sports fans, to watch this bantam rooster from the Deep South strut the stage and trash the "pointy-headed intellectuals" who he said had led the nation down the pathway to ruin.

A red-lettered banner with the slogan of Wallace's campaign theme, "Stand Up For America," was strung across the stage. A country band warmed up the crowd with the twangy vibrato of electric guitar, screechy violin, thumping drums and the close vocal harmonies of two big-haired blondes in mini-skirts, sisters Mona and Lisa Taylor. Sixteen years later, Lisa, thirty years younger than Wallace, became his third wife.

While Buffalo is some 900 miles north of Montgomery, Ala., Wallace's call, trumpeted under the heading of "Send Them a Message," was heard by many sons and daughters of Polish, Italian and Irish immigrants who toiled long, hard hours in the steel mills and auto plants, paid their taxes, saved for their children's educations and worried that all they were working for would go up in smoke in the chaos they saw around them.

Stephan Lesher, in his biography, "George Wallace: American Populist," said Wallace's appeal outside the South was not strictly due to racial animosity being expressed by Northern whites. Lesher wrote that *Newsweek* magazine's Joseph P. Cummings at the time described the Wallace appeal to voters in places like Buffalo as a far more complex phenomenon:

"In large Northern industrial centers, his (Wallace's) strength is among trade unionists and other lower-middle-class workers who have been hard-core Democrats backing liberal social legislation almost all their lives. Now they feel so threatened by the breakdown of 'law and order' or what he insists is 'softness' in coping with disorders that they are ready to vote against their own their own economic self interests for a Wallace, or preferably a Ronald Reagan, or, less enthusiastically, for Richard Nixon," Cummings wrote in *Newsweek*.

Wallace's huge crowd in Buffalo was swelled by a vocal cadre of several hundred protesting State University of New York at Buffalo students who came to show their opposition to what they saw as a racist candidate. When Wallace was introduced to thunderous cheers, the students booed and chanted. Then, as Wallace began to speak, they got up and walked out. An angry Wallace exhorted them to stay. But they continued their exodus, amid a cascade of boos from the rest of the crowd that came to support the candidate. My job as a reporter on the scene was to get quotes from the students, the more colorful the better, and phone them back in to the rewrite desk where they were to be incorporated into a story on the protests.

I will never forget the excitement I felt being on the inside of a history-making event, an excitement I still get covering presidential campaigns some 36 years later. The candidates come and go, and the issues change from cycle to cycle. But the roars of the crowds, the vibrations of the halls and the passion-flamed calls to arms by the candidates are like shots of adrenaline-fueled energy that course though my veins, sending tingly chills down my arms and bringing tears to my eyes.

I had similar experiences during the final weeks of the 2004 campaign. One that left a strong impression came when President Bush, after his third debate with Democrat John Kerry at Arizona State University, motorcaded over to the Bank One Ballpark, home of the Arizona Diamondbacks baseball team, where his supporters had gathered to watch the debate on the ballpark's big screen. As the presidential entourage, which included first lady Laura Bush, Bush daughters Barbara and Jenna and Arizona Republican Sen. John McCain and wife Cindy, walked onto the field from the home team dugout, I wasn't expecting the scene that greeted us. The three-tiered stadium, which holds 55,000 fans, was nearly filled with Bush fans - men, women and children - who waved flags and signs, stomped, cheered, screamed and whistled for a solid five minutes before they calmed down enough to let the president speak from home plate. McCain introduced Bush, recalling that the president beat him in the 2000 Republican presidential primaries. The crowd reacted with a wave of applause, causing a somewhat chagrined McCain to quip, "You didn't have to cheer that much."

Bush was visibly moved by the size of the crowd and its outpouring of affection and enthusiasm. He said he had been in a lot of ball parks before - he was once part owner of the Texas Rangers baseball team - but never one that contained so many people who were going to work the vote so he could win on Nov. 2, less than three weeks away."I can not thank you enough. It warms my heart and lifts my spirits," he said. At that point, Bush's re-election campaign was flagging, due in large measure to a poor performance in his first debate with Kerry in Coral Gables, Fla. some two weeks earlier. But he did as all politicians do when the going is tough: He confidently predicted victory. The rally seemed to give him renewed energy. He won Arizona handily, and the election itself, in a three-point squeaker.

Standing on the green grass along the first-base line, I looked up at the multitudes and recalled that thrill of excitement that came over me at the Wallace rally. And here I was, three decades and many campaigns later, still fueled by that old spark that I know will still be there long after I stop reporting. I thought about my job and how lucky I was to have been a witness to and recorder of so much history. After all, they say that daily news reporting is the first rough draft of history. I see it in more basic terms. Reporting is simple: You go places that other people don't go and you come back and tell them what you saw and heard.

In politics, and in reporting, things have a way of coming full circle. They did with Wallace. I only covered him from afar in 1968 when he ran for president. But 18 years later, I met up with the Alabama governor again, not as a reporter in the faceless crowds he spoke to hundreds of times in his stormy political career, but face to face in his office in Montgomery, where he was just seven months from retiring after four terms.

In May 1986, when I next met Wallace, I was a national political reporter for USA TODAY. I was sent to Alabama to do a story on the nasty primary fight being engaged in by two Democrats battling to succeed the legendary governor. I knew Wallace, by now wheelchair-bound from the 1972 gunshot wounds fired by a would-be assassin, Arthur Bremer, did few interviews, and would be highly unlikely to grant one to me, a perfect stranger. But in true journalistic tradition, I still gave it a try. I went to Wallace's veteran press secretary, Billy Joe Camp, who I knew slightly, and asked him if the governor would be willing to do an interview with me. Without hesitation, Camp said no.

But any reporter worth the paper in his notebook doesn't take the first no and walk away. I came back with a strategy. I said to Camp, "Tell the governor that the first big political event I ever covered was his 1968 rally in Buffalo, N.Y. He drew a big crowd and I was impressed with his strong speech, even in the face of some very tough protesters. Tell him we could talk about that, if he wants to." Camp was still skeptical, but said he would present my case to the governor if I could hang around a day or two. I called my desk back in Arlington, Va., outside of Washington, and told my editor that I needed to stay in Montgomery for at least two more days on the chance that I might get an interview with Wallace. The editor, like most editors, was hesitant to let a reporter sit somewhere for several days waiting for a story to develop with a chance that it might not develop at all. But the editor relented and I sat and waited.

The next morning I went to Wallace's office in the Alabama Statehouse and parked myself in the waiting room where two very pretty receptionists who looked like they could have been Miss Alabama beauty contestants sat at desks on either side of the door. One, whose nameplate on her desk said "Raylon," asked in the silkiest Southern drawl if she could help me. I told her I was there to see the press secretary, Mr. Camp. She told me to take a seat and picked up the phone and called Camp's office. "There's a Mr. Ben-a-det-to here to see Billy Joe. He'says he's from USA TODAY, the newspaper?" She seemed to be asking rather than telling. She hung up and turned to me with a big smile. "Billy Joe will be with y'all shortly."

Five minutes later, Camp, in black horn-rimmed glasses, came out with an unpromising look on his face. "I gave him your request. He didn't turn it down, but said he didn't think so. He's not feeling very well. He has a lot of pain, you know." I told Camp that since he didn't flatly say no, I would hang around in case he decides to do it. Camp shrugged and went back to his office, leaving me to read magazines and talk to the two pretty receptionists, who I referred to, privately of course, as "the bookends," neatly positioned on either side of the door to Wallace's office. At 4 p.m., Raylon said the governor had gone home, so there was no use waiting around any longer.

But just then, Camp appeared in the waiting room and said, "The governor will see you tomorrow morning. Fifteen minutes. No more." I was so excited, but tried to be cool. "I'll be here," I said. "And hey, thanks for your help." Camp replied, "It was the Buffalo mention that did it. He remembered that rally."

That evening, so excited that I could hardly contain myself, I went to the library to bone up on Wallace and construct my questions. With Wallace coming to the end of his tumultuous and controversial political career, I figured everyone would want to know how he assessed the job he did and what he achieved. History would provide its own judgments. The next morning, a smiling Raylon escorted me down a plush-carpeted corridor to the governor's office. Opening the door to a long narrow room, I saw Wallace, sitting in his wheelchair at the far end behind a huge desk that contained only two objects - a Bible and a plastic model of the B-29 bomber he flew in as an engineer during World War II. Flanking the desk were two flags, the American flag and the Alabama state flag. On a table behind him was a framed color photo of his third wife, Lisa, who left him shortly after the interview. Wallace, who looked tiny in a light gray suit and loosely knotted blue tie, gestured with the long cigar held tightly between the fingers of his left hand. "Come on in," he said in that familiar voice of his, which seemed softer, its hard edges filed down by the passage of time.

When I sat down on a chair next to his desk, the first thing he said to me was, "So you were at that rally in Buffalo, N.Y. in 1968?"

"Yes, sir, I was," I replied.

"I made a good speech, didn't I?" he asked somewhat wistfully, his misty eyes looking far beyond me, perhaps to that night in Buffalo.

"You sure did," I answered. "The crowd loved it."

It was easy to see he was in a lot of pain. The bullets fired into Wallace's body by Bremer in a Laurel, Md. shopping center parking lot while the governor was campaigning for president in 1972 left him paralyzed from the waist down. During the interview, he constantly shifted positions in his wheelchair trying to get comfortable, grimacing as he moved.

"Every year, the gunshot wounds take their toll," he said. "I have pain all the time. There's no medication for it."

Asked how he felt about Bremer, his assailant, Wallace said he hardly thought of him anymore unless someone mentioned his name. But the pain was a constant reminder, think of him or not.

"I don't hate him," Wallace said, implying that he had undergone some kind of spiritual transformation that allowed him to forgive.

With the Wallace era, which spanned 40 years of turbulent Alabama history, coming to a close, we talked about the upcoming primary election to succeed him. He said he had no regrets about choosing to step down, citing the pain as the main reason why he decided to call his political career to an end.

"Alabama will go right along," he said. "Nobody's indispensable."

Clearly, it was a far mellower Wallace than the one who burst on the national political scene in 1963 when he stood in the University of Alabama doorway to block racial integration ordered by the U.S. Justice Department, then headed by Attorney General Robert F. Kennedy. Told that he seemed more laid back, he said with a puff on his big cigar, "All of us mellow with age."

But mellow or not, Wallace still tried to put his own stamp on what happened, even though history might record it otherwise. He said his action to stop the integration had nothing to do with race. It was a matter of state's rights, he said.

"We were going to integrate the University of Alabama the next year. We wanted to put our own date on it, not the Justice Department," he said. "That's what the argument was - big government telling us what to do."

He said he didn't realize at the time that standing in the doorway would give him a "bad image" among blacks in other parts of the country.

"The public relations aspect of it was bad for me because it made it appear I was anti-black, when I was really anti-big government," he said. But flashes of the old, more prickly Wallace sparked when I tried to persist in the discussion of his record on race.

"There's no use to talk about it. It's over and gone," he whined. "Let's don't talk about it."

But he did want to talk about the fact that he was re-elected Alabama governor in 1982 with strong black support. He also noted that his son, George Jr., running for Alabama state treasurer that year, had won endorsement from a major black political group. His son won that election.

"We've gone through that transition period with such ease because we (whites and blacks) have been neighbors and friends all these years," Wallace said.

However, Wallace seemed to take on renewed energy when the conversation turned to what he clearly considered his glory days - his four presidential races in 1964, 1968, 1972 and 1976, - when he took obvious pleasure bashing the Ivy League liberals and leading the populist cause against big government, which he pronounced, "big govmint." But he recalled most fondly the 1968 campaign, his best showing, when his Independent Party candidacy carried five Southern states, four more, as he proudly pointed out, than Democrat Walter Mondale carried in a losing cause against Ronald Reagan in 1984.

That gave me an opening to discuss my coverage of his stop that year in Buffalo. He said he remembered that rally very well, not only for the enthusiasm of the crowd of supporters that greeted him, but also for the hospitality he received from some old fiends who lived there. He recalled staying at the Buffalo home of an old law school classmate who he said was Italian-American. He took obvious relish in talking about the great meal the family served and how friendly they were. "You're Italian, too, aren't you?" he asked. "Good people." Many years later, I tried to find out who the Buffalo family that hosted him was, but no one seemed to know. And Wallace by that time was dead, so I couldn't check with him. Maybe he made it up.

I mentioned that I remembered him exhorting the Buffalo protesters to come back and listen to him. He dismissed that with a wave of the hand. "They didn't know nothin'," he said.

Wallace said he had no regrets about running for president so many times and was buoyed by the belief that his runs helped cause a seismic shift in American politics. "I'm glad I did it," he said. "I'd do it again because I proved that a Southerner could carry a Northern state like Michigan."

Wallace shocked the political world when he won the 1972 Michigan Democratic primary over the party's eventual nominee, South Dakota Sen. George McGovern and Minnesota Sen. Hubert Humphrey, the former vice president. He also won Maryland, a border state. But for all practical purposes, his campaign was already over by the time those twin victories materialized A few days before the vote, Bremer shot him. And while voters went to the polls in Maryland and Michigan, Wallace was lying in a Silver Spring, Md. hospital recovering from surgery. Five bullets entered his body, one of which penetrated the spinal canal and severed a bundle of nerves that carried impulses from the lower body to the brain. He would never have another day without severe, debilitating pain. Some pundits believe that had he not been shot, he could have won the Democratic presidential nomination. Had he done that, would he have been able to beat Richard Nixon, the Republican incumbent? Probably not, but we'll never know.

While school busing to achieve racial integration was a big issue in the Michigan primary, Wallace, in the interview, contended that his primary wins in the North came not because of racism, but because "the average citizen has the same feeling about big government as we do. Reagan (in 1980) got elected on it," he said.

He also denied that much of his support in the North came from those who were anti-black. "Race was not an issue in the campaign," he insisted. "It was all over years ago."

Wallace said his biggest accomplishments during his long career were improving the Alabama education system and helping "conservatize" the nation. But when it was time for me to leave - I got at least double the 15 minutes I was first promised - Wallace returned to the rally in Buffalo 16 years earlier.

"So you were there," he said wistfully as I turned to leave.

"Yes, sir," I reiterated.

"I was good, wasn't I?" he pleaded.

I had to admit that he was, at least in style, if not in substance.

When I got out to Raylon's reception desk, she was on the phone.

She motioned me to wait. When she hung up, she asked if I could stop by the office later in the afternoon. She said she would have something to give me. I said I would and returned about 4 p.m. She handed me a big yellow envelope. "The governor said he wanted to give you this." Somewhat puzzled, I thanked her and opened it. It was a certificate commissioning me an honorary colonel in the Alabama militia, signed by George C. Wallace himself. All because I covered him in 1968 in Buffalo, an event of great glory in his mind.

In those early days in Buffalo I wanted to cover the city's major political figures, but as a raw rookie at the *Buffalo Evening News* I never was able to get the opportunity. The closest I got to covering then-Mayor Frank Sedita, a dapper, polite gentleman with a thin, gray moustache who often wore a flower in his lapel, was the night he came to speak before the Niagara Frontier Press Club, a loose gathering of Buffalo area journalists and public relations people who used any excuse to get together for a drink. I recall that Sedita came and gave some lofty speech about freedom of the press and all that. But you could tell he was anxious to get it over with so he could join in the cocktail chatter with the scribes. I wrote an article about the event that appeared in *The News-News,* the in-house newspaper written exclusively for *Buffalo Evening News* employees. The monthly paper featured such items as the scores of *The News* bowling league, the listing of loyal employees who had reached 25 years of service with the company and pictures of *News* couples celebrating their 50th wedding anniversary.

A typical item from *The News-News* circa 1970: "Stan Sobieraj, of Dispatch, recently returned from a week of fishing in Silver Lake and Lake Erie off Dunkirk. He forgot to mention whether he caught any fish. If you see him, ask."

Or this one: "Congratulations to Audrie Coon, of Accounting, for being the recipient of a special award for many years of service to her church. Audrie celebrated with a delightful weekend in Pennsylvania."

I wrote a lot of those items. And while it was pretty small-time stuff compared to covering the White House, I always enjoyed talking with the employees and coaxing the little stories out of them that everyone liked to read. *News* employees waited eagerly for each edition, and when it was late, we heard about it. During my tenure at *The News,* I was assigned to work in the Promotion Department, headed by the grandfatherly David

Peugeot and ramrodded by Joe Cardina, a street-smart former Army pilot who had a flair for producing publicity campaigns that caught the public eye and captured its fancy. Both men generously took me under their wings and patiently taught me the fundamentals of the work. Once instructed in the basics, they gave me the chance to try things on my own, perhaps sometimes long before I was ready. But both believed in learning by doing and sharing what they knew. For that, I will be eternally thankful to them. Peugeot is dead and Cardina is retired. But they remain heroes to me.

The Promotion Department was charged with touting various *News* features and personalities, all aimed at increasing the circulation of the paper. For example, we would write radio and TV ads calling attention to an upcoming series of articles in *The News* featuring beauty tips by actress Arlene Dahl, or the serialization of a new book by world explorer Thor Heyerdahl. We also would help create billboards, bus cards and posters that went on *News* delivery trucks calling attention to popular *News* human-interest columnists such as Bob Curran and Karen Brady or the paper's in-depth coverage of the Buffalo Bills. One poster I created that became the centerpiece of a *News* circulation campaign featured the pushy Lucy, of "Peanuts" comic strip fame, shouting "Be a Know-It-All. Read *The News*." It was so popular that the DayGlo posters were stolen off the trucks and out of the buses by youngsters who wanted to hang them in their rooms. We also had buttons made bearing Lucy's picture and the "Know-It-All" slogan, which were distributed around the community. They quickly became collectors items too, especially among the kids.

One of the most popular *News* promotions in the late 60s was the annual "Back-to-School Teen Fashion Show" held in mid-August in downtown's Shea's Buffalo Theater, the city's elegant movie palace on Main Street, now an historical landmark. The Buffalo, with its elegant dome far above the orchestra, was once the home of the popular 1940s radio quiz show, "Dr. IQ." The doctor gave out silver dollars as prizes to members of the audience who could answer his questions correctly. "Doctor, I have a lady in the balcony…" was the familiar intro to the program.

The News fashion show would feature a popular singer as well as the latest teen fashions modeled by young girls who would dance down the runway in their mini-skirts, puffy hairdos and white go-go boots. The show was free. All teens had to do to attend was send coupons found in the paper and a self-addressed stamped envelope to *The News* requesting the tickets. With popular teen heart throbs of the day such as Bobby Sherman ("Julie, Julie, Julie, Do You Love Me?") and Lou Christie ("Lightning Strikes") as the headliners, the 3,200 seats in Shea's Buffalo were always packed with screaming young girls right to the rear of the soaring balcony. My job: write copy for the ads promoting the show, interview the stars for news articles and stand backstage watching the models change from one skimpy outfit to another.

The News also sponsored a spelling bee, a photo contest, a crossword puzzle contest with cash prizes and a disabled children's summer camp at Butler Lake, all of which fell under the purview of our Promotion Department. But one of the biggest and most popular of *News* sponsorships was the annual Western New York Science Fair, where prizes were awarded to students with the best projects. In 1969, one of the winners was a young high school student from Cheektowaga by the name of Dale Hankin, who constructed a huge telescope in his back yard. At that time it was the biggest in the area except for the one on the roof of the Buffalo Museum of Science. I remember it well because 1969 was the year the first men landed on the Moon. And the week before the landing, *The News*, like all papers, looking for a local angle to complement a major national news event, sent me to interview young Dale, who was preparing his telescope to view the historic moment. As soon as I arrived in his back yard I could see this was no ordinary science project. Dale and his father had constructed a 12-foot high, cement-block building upon which the telescope was mounted. It rotated on an ingenious turntable made with roller-skate wheels. *The News* ran a big picture and article on young Dale and his telescope on the day before the Moon landing. I wrote it. So you might say I played my own minor part in that historical event.

I also got to interview a number of big-name entertainers who each summer would come to the Buffalo area to appear at Melody Fair, a huge tent theater in the suburb of North Tonawanda. The gimmick was we would give their shows free publicity if they would sit for an interview and pose for a picture reading *The News*. We would run the interview in the paper and use the photo as part of a promo that said, even the stars read *The News*. Among the headliners I interviewed in those days were Danny Kaye, Craig Stevens of Peter Gunn fame, singer Trini Lopez, Alexis

Smith, Mickey Rooney, Ann Miller, Janis Paige and Lucille Ball. The entertainer I remember most was Kaye, who was quite rude and short with the help in the restaurant where the interview took place. He was very picky about his food and constantly badgered the waitress about this or that not being just right. He also was impatient with the interview. It was quite a contrast to his kindly, comic on-stage persona. But while all of that was fun, I wanted to cover politics. And with *The News* well stocked with veteran political reporters such as George Borrelli, George Gates, Ray Hill and Jerry Alan, I decided it was time to move on. But not before stopping off for a year to get a master's degree in journalism from my alma mater, Syracuse University. I figured that the master's would help land that political reporting job I wanted. I was right.

REFERENCES

Lesker, Stephan. 1994. "George Wallace: American Populist," Boston, Addison-Wesley.

A Reporter Learns Some Lessons

Arriving on the Syracuse University campus in the fall of 1970, I found the tense atmosphere far different from the collegiate calm I remembered five years earlier. The school was awash with anti-Vietnam war and social justice fervor. The previous spring, Ohio National Guard troops fired into a crowd of Kent State University students protesting President Richard Nixon's decision to send American troops into Cambodia. The melee left four students dead. The dramatic pictures of young people lying in pools of blood triggered a massive wave of demonstrations, strikes and violence on college campuses across the country - a wave larger and more intense than any ever seen in American higher education history. At Syracuse, students erected barricades that closed off all entrances to the campus and began boycotting classes. They smashed windows and scrawled anti-war slogans in red paint on the walls of many campus buildings. More than 100 students staged a sit-in at Chancellor John Corbally's office and demanded that the university pay $100,000 to the Black Panther Defense Fund to bail out jailed Panther leader Bobby Seale. After more than 24 hours, the demonstration ended quietly, without any money being paid. Shortly after, with the campus still in turmoil, university officials cancelled the last six weeks of classes and final examinations, a move unprecedented in the Methodist-founded university's 100-year history.

But the summer recess did not seem to cool the student ardor for protest and reform. They picked up in September where they left off in May. But this time, the protest was not primarily the war, it was civil rights. Eight African-American Syracuse football players the previous spring had accused coach Ben Schwartzwalder of racial insensitivity, if not outright discrimination, and boycotted spring practice. They were later kicked off the team after refusing to sign a statement absolving the university of guilt. One of them was Al Newton, a star running back who led the Orange in rushing the previous two seasons. His decision to sit out his senior year probably cost him a professional football career. He was drafted by the Cleveland Browns, but never made it.

The 1970 home football season, minus the boycotting black players, began with a Sept. 26 home game against the Kansas Jayhawks, calling renewed attention to the racial boycott from the previous spring. When a sign-carrying throng of about 400 protesting students began marching toward Archbold Stadium, their path was blocked by 100 helmeted and masked riot police. A rock-and-bottle-throwing melee ensued. Pepper gas was sprayed and some students' heads were cracked by nightsticks. Arrests were made. Syracuse lost the football game, 31-14, but went on to a fairly successful 6-4 season without the black players.

Against that chaotic backdrop, I began my pursuit of a master's degree in journalism at Syracuse's Newhouse School of Public Communication, a school with a solid reputation in the news industry. At the ripe old age of 29, I was not there to protest. I was there to get an education. And I did. Many of the principles I use to guide me as a journalist I learned and honed at Syracuse. I had some wise and talented professors whose only goal was to make those in their charge the best journalists they could be. They had no political axes to grind, no social agenda to advance, no outsized egos they needed to project - at least none that was apparent to me. I can not say that for many college professors I come into contact with now as I travel to campuses around the country to speak to students. You can usually tell right away where most professors stand politically. Many make little attempt to hide it. Worse yet, they often try to convert their students to their cause, or at least give them only one side of the picture. If there is liberal bias in the media, the root cause could lie on college campuses today. Many professors today are part of the Baby Boom generation that cut its teeth on politics opposing the Vietnam war. And it has carried over into their teaching. I escaped college before that generational wave crested on faculties.

But what did I learn at Syracuse? To use a catch phrase that has become notorious today, and, in some corners, an object of derision: I learned to be thorough, fair and balanced. One very wise professor was Dr. Henry Schulte, a cigar-smoking former foreign correspondent with United Press International - once one of the nation's two largest news-gathering wire services - who later went on to become dean of the Newhouse School.

He put it this way: "You know you are doing a good job researching a story when the issue becomes grayer and grayer, not blacker and whiter."

In other words, at first blush, a news story may not be all that it seems. Therefore, it is incumbent upon the reporter to throughly examine all sides of the issue and make a complete and fair presentation. Sometimes, that means the story comes out a lot duller or less snappy than you thought going in.

But in today's fast-paced world of 24-hour television news channels and internet websites competing for audiences, newspapers facing shrinking readership and a society that puts a premium on scandal and celebrity, presenting the news in a fair and balanced way often is seen by those making media decisions as dull and boring. They want the stark shades of black and white that jazz up the story, not the more subtle tones of gray that might slow the beat. The blacker or whiter a story is, preferably blacker in tone and outlook, the greater its chance of getting big play. The dull news is relegated to the back pages, if it gets an airing at all. Truth? In a world of shifting values and the quest to disprove old verities, the truth has become relative, or at least flexible. Your vision of the truth might be different from my vision of the truth. My definition of "moral values" might be different from your definition of "moral values." So what makes you right and me wrong? And that's the way it goes.

Also at Syracuse, I was taught that public service was a noble profession, not a haven for scoundrels and crooks. In the eyes of my professors, politicians were not objects of automatic scorn to be trashed by the reporters covering them. Politicians, they told us, were people who had made a choice to serve the public in various offices of government. And not all of them were in there just to make themselves and their friends rich, the public be damned. We were taught in courses such as Public Affairs Reporting that while one of our main functions as reporters covering government would be to serve as a watchdog for the public, to make sure that its government was acting in its interests, it also was important that we inform the public about what its government was doing from day to day, the good along with the bad. Or as some journalism textbooks said about one of the key functions of the press, To inform the people so that they may be able to make decisions in a democracy based on full knowledge of events. Note that it said "inform" the people and provide them with "full knowledge" of events. It did not say that our role as reporters would be to influence them or persuade them. Our role would be to "inform" them by presenting them with as much information as possible. We also were cautioned that if we left out important information or overplayed the bad and downplayed the good, we would be creating a false impression with the public that its government was a hopeless mess. Sadly, that often is the case in the way we cover government today. When was the last time you read or viewed a story about a politician or a government agency that was doing a good job? Such stories are few and far between. It's not because there is little good to report. We just skip good work by governments as routine, something to be expected. Yet, we do not have to look far to find reports about those people or programs that are falling short. We simply need more balance.

Often, you hear people say that the reason why the media overemphasize the negative is that "bad news sells." But good news sells, too. I get more mail from readers of my column when I write something positive about the government and politicians than I do when I write something negative. People enjoy good news, too. Moreover, I find it more fun to write.

You Can Go Home Again

With my Syracuse graduation nearing, it was time to find a job. But with an economic recession in full tilt that spring of 1971 - *Time* magazine published a cover of a college graduate in cap and gown pumping gas - jobs were hard to come by. My old newspaper, the *Buffalo Evening News,* still was not ready to make me a political reporter. And interviews at the *Providence Journal*, the *Boston Globe* and *Newsday* did not pan out. But thanks to Mason Taylor, the politically savvy executive editor of the Gannett-owned *Daily Press* and *Observer-Dispatch* in my hometown of Utica, N.Y., I was offered a job of covering city government. I had misgivings at first about going back home, but it was a job, and a job doing what I wanted to do. So I took it, still wondering whether going back home was the right decision. Over time, however, I came to appreciate my good fortune. Not only did I have a job covering politics, but I had it in a town where many of the political players were already familiar to me, putting me at an advantage. I knew the current mayor, Democrat Dominick Assaro, a dapper Italian-American funeral director who that year was running for re-election to a second two-year term. His underdog Republican rival was a political newcomer, Michael Caruso, an affable, rough-cut businessman whose family ran a successful cheese-making factory in Utica. Also on the political docket that year was a race for Oneida County executive between Democrat Bill Bryant and Republican incumbent Harry Daniels.

Coming on the job in July, those two races were about to shift into high gear. And I got a chance to cover both of them. I was in heaven. My first by-lined story, which came on July 2, was a "man-on-the-street" piece. On July 1, a new state sales tax on food, known derisively as the "hot dog tax," went into effect. My job was to go out on the street and ask people how they liked it. Of course, nobody did. But it gave people a chance to vent. Readers loved it. It just reinforced what they had been thinking and saying themselves. The story got big play. "Rockefeller is a bum," said one guy I questioned on a downtown street, referring to New York Gov. Nelson Rockefeller, who pushed the tax. When merchants would collect the tax, they would say to their customers, "And two more cents for Rocky."

But the first story I wrote that caused readers to stand up and take notice was the one that exposed how poorly city street-cleaning crews were performing their jobs. In the fall of 1971, with the mayoral race getting hot, many Utica residents were complaining that the Department of Public Works (DPW) was doing a sloppy job of picking up leaves and trash left at curbsides in residential sections of the city. Weeks would go by in some neighborhoods without any pickup. The subject became a hot topic of conversation on a popular afternoon talk show hosted by Ralph Romano, a hard-nosed veteran radio personality who spoke the people's language. It seemed that in those days everyone listened to Ralph Romano. And it seemed that Romano, or at least most of his callers, were out to get Mayor Assaro. If you walked through City Hall you could hear the show emanating from every office, and employees fretting that Romano's tirades would cost them their jobs if Assaro lost.

With each caller seeming to have a horror story to tell about the incompetence of city street-cleaning crews, I decided to go out and have a look for myself. One day, I got in my 1968 Camaro and covertly followed several crews from the beginning of their shifts at 8 a.m. until they punched out at 4:30 p.m., keeping a time log and diary of what I saw. Then I wrote it up and the *Daily Press* published it the next morning. The Sept. 16, 1971 story, under the headline, "A Study of Inefficiency," caused a sensation. Here is how it went:

"Street-cleaning crews operating in East Utica met with a series of work delays yesterday.

"One four-man crew working near James Street and Brookside Avenue stood idle for more than an hour waiting for trash trucks to return from the dump.

"Parked on Brookside were a street-sweeping tractor and payloader. Their motors were left running during most of the wait.

"When a dump truck finally arrived at 11:45 a.m., the crew jumped on and went to lunch. In the meantime, another dump truck arrived on the scene and waited until the crew came back. The driver said the delay (in getting back) was due to getting the tarpaulin situation straightened out. (Crews had been under fire for not using tarpaulins on the trucks to cover the trash, as required by law.)

"A second crew working yesterday in the Leeds and Eagle Street area was observed using a tarpaulin to cover trash in trucks, as required by law, but a member of the same crew was seen pushing trash into a sewer. Among the items were a soda can and sticks. A block away, on Kossuth Avenue, a crew was seen cleaning sewers with a large vacuum truck.

"Also observed in the 1200 block of Leeds Street was a crewman discarding into a dump truck a 'No Parking At Any Time' sign that had been loosened" when the truck backed into it.

"An ordinance requesting $12,500 to replace and repair city signs was referred to committee by the Common Council last night.

"At 1:40 p.m., the crew that had been idle on Brookside had filled a dump truck with trash while working on South Street near Rudolph Place. The truck was covered with a tarpaulin and left for the dump. The remaining four workmen waited for 25 minutes for an empty truck to return. Work then resumed."

The article was a bombshell. It was the talk of the Romano show that afternoon. Mayor Assaro was embarrassed and livid, not only at me, but at his DPW chief, a friendly fellow by the name of Jim Benedetto, no relative of mine. Caruso, Assaro's opponent, used the article as ammunition against the mayor, noting that it proved what he had been saying all along - the DPW was incompetent. The public furor reached crisis proportions. Assaro, forced to do something, fired his public works chief and shook up the street-cleaning staff. But it was too late. That and a number of other issues helped to defeat the mayor. In a way, I felt a little guilty. I liked Dick Assaro. He was a gentleman, and he was always nice to me. His family and mine had been friends for many years. But I called it as I saw it, which was my job. And I learned right then and there, early in my career, the lesson that my Utica editor Tony Vella taught me: The names you write in the paper have real people attached to them, and the words you print affect their lives.

I reported what I saw as the truth. But it had consequences. While I learned quickly that I had power, I never felt quite comfortable wielding it in ways that hurt people, whether I liked them or not, and whether they deserved it or not. And I still don't. But it is part of the job, a part I accept.

Here I was in Utica holding down my first political reporting job and feeling pretty big. The local radio and televisions stations, most of which did not have reporters assigned full time to cover City Hall, would pirate my stories. It was not unusual to wake up in the morning and hear my written words coming back at me on the radio news reports, without attribution to me or the newspaper. The radio newscasters would just rip the stories out of the paper and read them as if they had reported them themselves. Even today, the practice continues to be widespread in localities all across the country.

I learned that while covering government and politics for a main newspaper in a small or medium-size city, a reporter achieves some standing in the community, for better or for worse. My readers sometimes thought that I had magical powers and with the wave of a pen or with the flourish of a typewriter key - in those days, we still wrote our stories on typewriters and submitted them on paper, with carbon copies - I could get the city to repair a pothole on their street, plant a tree in their front yards or install a traffic light at the busy intersection their children had to cross on their way to school. While many such requests would come to me, which I would pass on to their council member, the fact that the people saw me on their side was a compliment and suggested a degree of faith, trust and confidence they then were willing to place in their news media. Some of that trust and confidence has faded in recent years.

Aside from covering the day-to-day workings of City Hall - the City Council meetings, the Zoning and Planning Board hearings and public events that the mayor attended - I also was encouraged by my editors to undertake projects and investigations. One of them, looking into the practices of the Utica Urban Renewal Agency as it acquired private property for demolition in the downtown area, won a Frank W. Tripp Award, then the most prestigious award for reporting in Gannett Co. newspapers across the country. The investigation found that federal regulations in acquiring property were not always followed and that some of the acquisitions were sweetheart deals for friends of people making the agency decisions. The series caught the attention of higher-ups in Gannett, and led to my eventual promotion to the *Gannett News Service* news bureau in Albany, where I went on to cover state government and politics. My more immediate reward was a wood-mounted plaque and $500, which my wife and I used to remodel the outdated bathroom of a house we had just bought. In those days you could easily do it for that amount.

Another attention-getting project I initiated in those early days in Utica dealt with the growing blight of the city's once solidly middle-class Cornhill neighborhood. The 1950s and '60s exodus to the suburbs caused many poorer families or absentee landlords to cheaply buy Cornhill homes, changing the character of the neighborhood. Over time, many of the properties fell into disrepair, abused by tenants and neglected by landlords mostly interested in milking the properties for profit. By the mid-1970s, many of the homes were abandoned, becoming havens for drug addicts and targets for vandalism and arson. Moreover, the city, which had become the owner when the landlords stopped paying taxes, was slow in demolishing the eyesores. Residents of the neighborhood who were doing their best to keep their properties up were growing angrier by the minute. One day, I decided to make an accounting of just how many houses in the neighborhood were abandoned. No one had ever done it. So I got in my car and with my six-year-old daughter Kristen as my clerk, drove up and down streets in Cornhill surveying the unoccupied buildings. I forgot how many we found, but it was more than 100. The story, which led the Sunday newspaper, caused a furor. But when the dust died down, it helped spur efforts to speed up demolition. Some private companies even volunteered to help.

Another story that got results was one that reported that Utica's downtown sign ordinance, which limited the size and location of signs in front of businesses on the city's main commercial streets, was not being enforced. A photo taken by one of our photographers showed the city's main street, Genesee Street, a jumble of unsightly signs of different sizes, shapes and color hanging over the sidewalks. The article triggered a flurry of civic pride by a group of downtown merchants led by Utica Floral Shop owner Chris Brown to voluntarily remove their overhanging signs and place them on the facades of their buildings. I wrote an article on that, and other merchants up and down the street followed. The city began enforcing its sign code and soon most of downtown was in compliance. Genesee Street looked a lot neater. Today, however, some 30 years later, Utica's downtown section is only a shadow of what it once was, with most of the merchants gone and store signs few and far between.

During my five years of reporting in Utica, I covered three mayors - Assaro, Caruso and Edward A. Hanna. All were basically nice guys with whom I jousted on occasion. But Hanna, a former Marine, self-made millionaire businessman and son of Lebanese immigrants, was by far the most colorful, volatile and controversial. He came along in 1973, but had dabbled in politics for a long time before. He was a one-term Democratic state Assemblyman and served as city parks commissioner in the late 1950s. Under his leadership, many said the parks never looked so neat and beautiful. Hanna was a severe taskmaster and a stickler for neatness, a trait carried by many ex-Marines. Park lawns were well manicured, colorful flower beds were planted and maintained in public areas and fountains that had not worked for years began spurting arching streams of water again. When police caught youths vandalizing the parks, they did not turn them over to the courts. They turned them over to Hanna, who called in their parents, read them the riot act and put the kids to work in parks on Saturdays clearing brush, emptying trash cans and pulling weeds. Not a parent complained. He had his own program of community service.

In 1973, with Utica, like most upstate New York cities, in severe economic decline, Hanna decided to run for mayor. For many years he had been associated with Utica's Democratic political machine led by Rufus P. Elefante, a local trucker, whose political power dwindled in the wake of a late-1950s state probe of vice, crime and corruption in the city. Elefante was never indicted, but many of his close friends and associates did prison time, including several city government officials and high-ranking members of the police department. Hanna, rather than run as a Democrat, and risk being tainted as part of the old political machine, decided to campaign as an independent reformer. He won popular support when he said he would finance his campaign with his own money and refuse any donations. Moreover, he pledged that if elected, he would refuse his mayoral salary - then $25,000 a year - and serve for $1. Most Uticans, who considered frugality a virtue, liked that. Hanna ran a bombastic campaign, buying time on the radio to make long-winded denunciations of the current regime. He quickly became the darling of the local radio talk shows. And he won easily, unseating Republican Caruso after one two-year term.

Hanna's first act as mayor was to remove the door from his City Hall office, leaving it open for the public to walk in and see him at any time. He also put a sign above his couch that said, "The Town's Living Room." Every day the office would be mobbed with job-seekers, citizens with complaints and hangers-on who loved being near the seat of power. The traffic became so chaotic that the door went up after three days. But Hanna's unusual gesture toward openness won nationwide publicity. Reporters from out-of-town newspapers - the *New York Times* and the *Washington Post* among them - came to town to write about this new maverick mayor who professed to be a true man of the people.

Hanna, elated by the national publicity, quickly dubbed the Utica newspapers his enemy, referring publicly to the *Daily Press* as "The Daily Mess," and the *Observer-Dispatch* as "The Observer-Disgrace." The public loved it. But Hanna managed the city with the deft hand of a lumberjack. He once, in a fit of pique, fired the entire Public Works Department and called *Washington Post* reporter Bill Claiborne at home in the middle of the night to come up to Utica to report on it. Claiborne, who had come to Utica from the *Post's* New York bureau to write about Hanna's antics, said it was not unusual to receive calls from the upstate mayor at all hours telling of his latest outrageous move in hope of gaining more national news coverage. Hanna was a charter subscriber to the theory that any publicity, no matter how bad, was better than no publicity at all.

In 1975, Hanna got so caught up in his notoriety that he decided he would be an independent candidate for the U.S. Senate seat then held by the venerable liberal Republican, Jacob Javits. Hanna made his announcement in a crystal-chandeliered, red-carpeted ballroom at the posh Plaza Hotel in New York City. I was sent down to cover it. The New York political reporters who showed up thought it was a joke. And when Hanna, with his attractive wife Ellen on his arm, made his grand entrance by walking down the center aisle wearing a black velvet suit and velvet shoes, they were convinced. You could hear their snickers as he passed by. The Hanna Senate campaign never went much beyond the press conference.

Hanna and I had our moments of tension and contention, but he basically thought I was fair and treated me much better than some of my colleagues. It was he who opened up the Urban Renewal records to me that were instrumental in constructing and writing the series of articles that won the Tripp Award. Without his cooperation, I could have never

34   *You Can Go Home Again*

written the story in the concise detail I did. And he would sometimes tell me privately that he liked something I wrote. But he would never say so publicly lest it mar his tough-guy image, which he carefully and skillfully crafted.

In addition to reporting on government and politics in Utica, I also wrote a weekly human-interest column. "Around and About." The title was taken from newspaperman Damon Runyon's description of a guy who was street smart: "He is a fellow you often see around and about," wrote Runyon, a clever chronicler of kind-hearted, savvy Broadway gamblers, touts and small-time crooks in a 1930s, harmlessly hip world that never really existed. His work was memorialized in the Broadway musical, "Guys and Dolls."

The column was the brainchild of my city editor, Frank Tomaino, a smart newspaperman who loves the city of Utica and its people. Even in retirement that love affair blooms in his weekly column about the city's history, one of the most well-read-and-talked-about features in the *Observer-Dispatch*. He detected a similar love in me and encouraged me to go out and recognize those people we pass by every day, but seldom stop to talk to, and tell their stories. So with Tomaino's blessing, I began to write about people in the community who seldom if ever got their names in the paper, but nonetheless were worth knowing and celebrating. People like Red Castilla, dubbed "The Mushroom King" by his friends because of his uncanny skill for going into the woods with an empty bushel basket and coming out with his container filled to the brim with tender chunks of wild mushrooms. I found Castilla one rainy night in his usual hangout, the bar of the American Legion hall in the blue-collar village of Frankfort, just outside of Utica. Many residents there worked at the Remington Arms factory in nearby Ilion. When I walked into the bar, I was greeted like the movie scene when the gunslinger walks into the saloon. The piano stopped, conversations went silent and all eyes turned toward the door. "I'm looking for Red Castilla," I called out. The bartender looked around the silent room and turned to me. "You a cop?" he asked.

Readers liked those columns featuring modest, everyday people doing interesting things that deserved recognition. Although I have no scientific studies to prove it, I will bet, judging from the public responses I received, that they were far-better read than any of my meticulously crafted political reports.

Once, after being tipped off by a priest, I wrote about 60 students from St. Agnes School who attended the funeral of Thomas "Little Tommy" Chrehan when they heard he had died leaving no relatives. They took it on as a project to practice the virtues of charity and compassion. And I followed up with a column on how Little Tommy's pals at Bengee's Bar, near where he lived in a one-room walkup, took up a collection to buy him a gravestone. Big burly guys with fists like sledge hammers would gingerly slip nickels and dimes through a narrow slot in the top of a glass jar on the bar. "For Little Tommy" they would say. The small, rectangular granite stone they bought read, "Thomas Crehan, Died March 1, 1976, Erected By All His Friends." There was even money left over to buy flowers.

Another column featured a guided house tour led by Mrs. Lucy Wente, then-owner of Lindy's Tourist Home, a longtime Utica fixture on Genesee Street that most Uticans drove past many times, but never visited. The converted brick mansion was amazingly comfortable, almost luxurious. Its 20 spacious guest rooms and 12 baths featured fancy oak woodwork, mahogany beds and dressers and old oriental rugs. Most of Mrs. Wente's overnight guests at that time were older people. But she said she did cater to some younger folks, too, although for them there were rules.

"If a young woman wants to have a male guest visit," she said. "she can meet him in the television sitting room. Anyone who sends a daughter to stay here knows that it is a well-run place."

From time to time I would use my column to record the passing of a Utica-area institution such as the neighborhood movie theaters with their Saturday matinees for kids - three cowboy movies, a serial, a cartoon, a newsreel and previews of coming attractions - all for 20 cents. Sometimes they would give away door prizes like a Schwinn bicycle or a wooden-mallet croquet set. I never won anything, but one of my buddies, David Vidoni, won a puppy, which he appropriately named "Lucky" and kept for many years.

One East Utica institution celebrated in my column is Ventura's Restaurant, which is still operated by Rufus Ventura Jr. I wrote about his father, a rabid New York Yankee fan who flew a Yankee flag from a pole on his restaurant's roof. When the Yankees won, the flag would fly at full staff, half-mast for a loss. Passers-by could look up and instantly know how the Yankees made out that day. Some guys would drive by just to find out. One night in 1974, I went down to Ventura's and watched a Yankees-Red Sox game on television at the bar with Rufus Sr. and an assortment of neighborhood regulars, all of whom were die-hard Yankee fans. I wrote about their sarcastic banter in my column. Late in the game, a Red Sox runner slid into third base in a close play. "He's out!" shouted the Yankee fans in unison.. "He's safe," called out Tony Polera. "What's the matter? Can't you guys see?" The gang broke into raucous laughter. Tony, who was wearing dark glasses, was blind.

While Buffalo was the place where I first encountered big time politicians like George Wallace, Utica was where I actually got to meet and interview some of them. In covering the 1971 mayoral election, I came into contact with two Democrats who ran for president in 1972 - then-New York Mayor John Lindsay and Maine U.S. Sen. Edmund Muskie. Both came to Utica to attend fundraisers for the incumbent Democratic mayor, Dick Assaro. Lindsay, with his movie-star good looks, was then in his second term as New York mayor. Spurned by his own Republican Party as too liberal when he ran for re-election in 1969, he won a second term on the Liberal Party line. By the time he came to Utica, two years later, he was looking at running for president as a Democrat.

Lindsay's arrival was staged with the pomp and ceremony befitting a movie star, not a politician, at least not in those days. With searchlights scanning across the dark, early autumn sky, and a fancy-dressed, cheering crowd of admirers gazing upward, Lindsay arrived in a chattering helicopter that touched down on the 18th green of the Valley View Golf Course. Amid shouts of "Welcome, Mr. President!" and "We love you!" Lindsay was whisked into the clubhouse where the fundraiser was held. I got a very brief interview with him in which he said nice things about Assaro, but remained aloof about his presidential plans. Lindsay did go on to enter the Democratic presidential primaries in 1972, running a campaign based too heavily on taking advantage of his telegenic good looks and not enough on his remedies for the nation's ills. His support failed to materialize and after a miserable sixth-place showing in the Wisconsin primary, he dropped out of the race. Theodore H. White, in his book, "The Making of the President 1972," wrote this about the failed

Lindsay effort: "Rarely has so eloquent a spokesman for profoundly important a cause (social justice) presided over so blundering a political campaign."

Muskie was the other national politician I covered in Utica. At that time, he was the frontrunner for the 1972 Democratic presidential nomination. He had been Hubert Humphrey's vice presidential running mate in 1968. His dogged middle-of-the-road moderation, in contrast to Humphrey's left-leaning liberalism, impressed many Democrats who saw him as a winner. It was with the mantle of favorite that he came to Utica. When Muskie flew into Oneida County Airport aboard a small private plane, Assaro, the beneficiary of the visit, was there to meet him. I was there too, invited by Assaro to ride in the car with him, offering me a chance to get an exclusive interview.

The interview was a bust. Muskie seemed to be in a sour mood and snapped his answers at me. He actually got angry when I asked him questions about his own presidential run. I was no political expert, but I wondered if this is what he would do when the presidential race really got hot and the questions started coming from reporters far more skilled and seasoned than me. The interview was prophetic. Muskie, in his campaign a few months later, projected a surly, suffer-no-fools persona and a short fuse that exploded in Manchester, N.H., all but killing his presidential bid. It came in an emotional speech one week before the New Hampshire primary, delivered from the back of a flatbed truck. With large flakes of wet snow falling all around him, and gathering on his wiry hair and thick eyebrows, Muskie, angrily denounced William Loeb, the right-wing publisher of the *Manchester Union Leader*, as a "gutless coward" for printing attacks on his wife and accusing the candidate of derogatorily referring to French-Canadians as "Canucks." As Muskie unleashed his diatribe, his voice broke. Some interpreted it as a sob. Others reported that he was crying. Whatever it was, "It changed people's minds about me," Muskie said later. He won the New Hampshire primary with 45 percent of the vote, but his nine-percentage-point margin over second-place finisher George McGovern was deemed by the media as too small for a neighbor from Maine. Muskie himself had predicted he would do much better. It was the beginning of the end for him.

Continuing on the trail of big-time politicians, in late June 1972 I was sent to Mineola, N.Y., the Nassau County seat on Long Island, to cover a press conference being held there by then-Vice President Spiro Agnew. With 1972 an election year, Agnew, seeking to score political points for the Nixon-Agnew re-election bid, came to announce the New York counties that would be eligible for federal disaster assistance money to repair damage suffered during the flooding triggered a week earlier by Hurricane Agnes.

Agnes was a nasty storm that after wreaking havoc on the South, moved out to sea off the North Carolina coast only to regain strength and sweep northward to Long Island and into upstate New York. Oneida County, where Utica is located, experienced some serious flooding and was expected to be one of the counties on the list for federal help. So I was sent to report on it.

Agnew, looking immaculate in a silver-blue suit, crisply starched white shirt with French cuffs, his gray hair tightly slicked back close to his head, walked in and took a seat at a table in front of the room. His press secretary, Victor Gold, stepped to the microphone and told the reporters gathered, most of the them from the New York City media, that the vice president would only answer questions on the topic of the hurricane. All other subjects, Gold said, would not be allowed. The announcement triggered immediate grumbling among reporters who had come to quiz the vice president about the campaign. They could not care less about the flood money. Moreover, the U.S. Supreme Court that day had handed down a landmark decision, Furman v. Georgia, that in effect put a moratorium on the death penalty and forced state legislatures to redraw their capital punishment laws. The New York reporters were champing at the bit to get the pro-death penalty vice president's reaction to that, as well.

When Agnew finished announcing the disaster assistance, he opened the floor for questions. The first one asked was about the death penalty. Agnew glowered, his steel-blue eyes just slits, and declared the question out of bounds. A murmur rippled through the reporters, and the second question also was on the death penalty. Obviously miffed, Agnew said through clenched teeth that the conference would end unless the questions went back to the topic at hand. They didn't. And Agnew walked out, leaving behind one irate bunch of New York reporters who trashed him in their stories the next day. But the bad publicity didn't hurt. The Nixon-Agnew ticket easily carried New York over Democrats George McGovern and Sargent Shriver.

Earlier that month, McGovern, running in the New York Democratic presidential primary, made a Saturday-morning campaign appearance in the parking lot of the New Hartford Shopping Center just outside of Utica. A rookie reporter at the time, my heart skipped a beat when I saw the pack of big-shot political reporters that included stars such as David Broder of the *Washington Post*, Jack Germond of the *Gannett News Service*, R.W. Apple, Jr. of the *New York Times*, Walter Mears of the *Associated Press* and then radio reporter Connie Chung pile off the bus and take places in front of the stage. I didn't know that a little more than a decade later I would become part of that pack.

Dante Tranquille, the Observer-Dispatch's veteran chief photographer, was one of my heroes. As a youngster I marveled at beautiful pictures he took, especially the football pictures that the paper spread across all eight columns of the Sunday sport page - pictures taken at Syracuse and Colgate University football games. I used to cut them out and paste them in a scrapbook, one of which I still have. The Tranquille football photos stick in my memory for the way they seemed to make the rough-and-tumble action look like graceful ballet. Tranquille, a revered man in the community, always had time to give young reporters like me a kind word and a bit of gentle advice. A cigar forever clenched between his teeth, he was the picture of cool, in a hot sea of panic. "Don't worry about it," was his favorite phrase. As his name said - tranquil. But what I remember most was Dante's big heart. One night, Nick Trimboli, the overworked-and-probably-underpaid Utica-area reporter for the *Syracuse Herald-Journal,* came into the *O-D* news room looking for Tranquille. "Dan! Dan!" he called spotting him coming out of the darkroom. "Can you help me out? Can you help me out? I was supposed to get a picture down at that City Hall news conference and I missed it. My paper is screaming for a picture. Can you help me out?" Tranquille turned around, walked into the darkroom and emerged with a photo. He handed it to Trimboli. Trimboli looked at it, thanked him profusely and ran out. "I owe you one, Dan," he said on his way out the door. Tranquille never uttered a word in the whole transaction. He was that kind of a guy.

One non-political celebrity I got a chance to cover in Utica - if "cover" is the right word to describe it, was actor Paul Newman. He had come to Utica to film scenes for a movie, "Slap Shot," which he was starring in. The film was about minor league hockey which at that time was being played in Utica. So Newman and his Hollywood crew had come to town to shoot some game footage in its natural setting. My editor sent me over to the Memorial Auditorium to get an interview with Newman. Sounded like a piece of cake. I never got it, even though he rudely kept me waiting for most of the day. Angry at the brusque treatment, I sat down and wrote a column that wound up being not only a jab at Newman, but also a tip of the hat to politicians. I still feel the same way, nearly 30 years later. Here is how it appeared in the *Observer-Dispatch* nearly 30 years ago:

"Give me a choice between interviewing a movie star and interviewing a politician and I'll take the politician every time.

"Politicians, despite their faults, are real people who because of the nature of their jobs can't afford to stray too far from reality and close personal contact with those who put them where they are. But movie stars are a different breed. The have trouble determining where the unreal world of film ends and the real world begins.

"Take Paul Newman, for example. He so prefers the security and comfort of his unreal world that he hesitates to come in direct contact with those from outside the bubble in which he encloses himself. And on the rare occasions when he does, it is only under controlled circumstances with strict ground rules.

"Unlike a politician, Paul Newman would never dream of taking a walk down Genesee Street to say hello to the many Uticans who've plunked down thousands of dollars to see his films. Instead, Newman, while in Utica, sequestered himself in his dressing-room van and threw an occasional wave (from the window) to a swooning female.

"When word came last Friday morning that Paul Newman and crew of 100 were at the Auditorium to begin filming some scenes for 'Slap Shot,' I was sent over to do a story. Photographer Jim Armstrong came along for the pictures. We arrived at 8:30 a.m. and were told Newman was in his van. I knocked on the door, which was answered by a tall, attractive woman wearing a beige pantsuit. I found out later that she was Nancy Dowd, who wrote the screen play. I identified myself and said I would like to talk briefly with Mr. Newman, at his convenience.

" 'You'll have to see our publicity man,' she said tersely and closed the door.

"A bit miffed, I went off to find the guy whose job it is to get all the free press coverage for the movie he can get. I was introduced to Jim Campbell, a big man with a southern drawl who looked like a retired heavyweight contender. Campbell was friendly, but not very encouraging about our chances for a picture and interview.

" 'There have been some last-minute changes in the script and he won't feel very much like talking,' Campbell said.

"He added that Newman doesn't often grant interviews, anyway. Nonetheless, Campbell tried to persuade some people that Newman should take a few minutes, answer a couple of questions and take a picture, but he wasn't having much luck.

"Suddenly, Newman appeared at the door of the van - sunglasses, cap, corduroy jeans, high boots and needing a shave. He stepped down and began heading for another van. I made a move toward him, but Campbell said, 'Not now.'

"So we let Newman disappear again. Another 20 minutes passed. Through the window we could see Newman sitting in the van wearing a tee-shirt and passing papers to someone. When he finally emerged, he made no attempt to talk to us, although he knew we were waiting for him. Instead, he ducked into another dressing room inside the Auditorium.

"Campbell, now getting uncomfortable, went and talked to someone else and returned to tell us it would be a few minutes yet. His optimism was waning.

"He doesn't want his picture taken until he gets into character for the scene. He is sensitive because he needs a shave. He's busy learning his lines. He's tired. We've been shooting for 68 days."

"'Couldn't I just ask one question?' I asked. 'I could show Utica readers that the guy is actually here and knows how to talk." The PR man shrugged his shoulders.

"But Newman insulated himself with a wall of burly hockey players and a phalanx of lights and equipment. I stuck around anyway, hoping that my persistent presence would eventually cause him to relent just to get rid of me. No luck. The only thing he consented to was to have the photographer come in and take some pictures while he ran though his scene. However, no flashbulbs could be used.

"Can you imagine President Ford telling press photographers that no flashbulbs can be used?

"Newman ran though his lines - three or four sentence of rhetoric that included expletives that any kid could have learned in five minutes. This was the script change that upset him?

"Armstrong took his pictures and took off. Newman went along his merry way. And as I said before, give me a politician, anytime."

The day the Newman column appeared, I got a lot of irate calls from his many female fans who berated me for treating their heart throb so shabbily. One questioned my credentials to criticize such a big star. And another said flat out that the reason why I was so tough on Newman was because I was jealous of his good looks. "You wish," the caller said. Anyway, Newman shouldn't have taken his work so seriously. "Slap Shot" was not one of his more memorable films. I admit, however, that I saw it and liked it.

Other celebrities I covered or interviewed in those early Utica days had their moments of difficulty, but none reached the arrogance of Newman. Bernadette Devlin, the fiery socialist from Ireland, spoke in November 1974 at Hamilton College in nearby Clinton, and proved to be a delightful, albeit intense, interview subject.

Devlin, then 26, had made world headlines fighting police on the barricades in Belfast during the 1969 riots protesting British rule in Northern Ireland, a bitter battle that continues today. She served four months in prison for assaulting police and inciting a riot. Later, while serving in the House of Commons as a member of the British Parliament, she leaped out of her seat and attacked, with kicks and claws and screams, the British Home secretary who was making a speech against her cause.

But the Devlin I met showed none of those characteristics, at least outwardly. I described her this way:

"She looks like a little girl whose mother brushed her hair before letting her out the door. Her white blouse, blue sweater and brushed denim jeans were as neat as a Catholic schoolgirl's uniform....Her angelic face, green eyes and polite manner would be welcomed with open arms by any young man's mother. And her soft Irish brogue belied the intensity of her words. 'If someone tries to stand on my neck again, I'll be left with no other option but to fight them,' she said very quietly."

Do you remember the song "Bernadette" by the Four Tops? I don't think the syncopated rhythm-and-blues quartet had Bernadette Devlin in mind when they sang that 1967 Motown hit.

No remembrance of my early days in reporting would be complete without a tip of the hat to my older colleagues who lived up to the often exaggerated, if not inaccurate, image of hard-drinking newsmen made famous in movies of the 1930s and 1940s by actors such as Pat O'Brien in "The Front Page," James Cagney and James Gleason in "Come Fill the Cup," Humphrey Bogart in "Deadline-USA," Clark Gable in "It Happened One Night" and Lee Tracy in a lot of films . I remember in my early days at the *Buffalo Evening News* that editor Bud Wacker would send a copy boy across the street to the Nimrod, a long, narrow, dark saloon, to find a reporter he needed. He sent a kid rather than call because the bartender who answered the phone would always say, "He ain't here."

One night in the Utica newsroom, Executive Editor Mason Taylor came out of his glass-enclosed office and rounded up several reporters to come downstairs with him. When we got to the lobby, he walked us out to the rear of the building where two men at the back of a huge truck were piling case-upon-case of beer on the sidewalk. Taylor ordered us to haul the cases upstairs. We used the elevator, of course, but when we finished there were about 50 cases of Maximus Super beer piled high in front of the newsroom. Why? The West End Brewing Company, brewer of Utica Club and Matt's Premium beers, was coming out with a new product, Maximus Super, which was being aimed at the college audience. You could drink at 18 in New York back then. West End was looking for the Utica newspapers to provide some free publicity for their new brew. Once the beer was in the newsroom, Taylor ordered us to put a case under the desk of every reporter and editor, including himself. Those coming in to work in the morning got a free surprise. But it did little good. Maximus Super flopped.

One more Taylor story: One hot summer night, the guys in editor Phil Spartano's Sports Department decided that it was too warm in the newsroom to work without a cold beer. So they put ice in a waste basket, dropped in their beer cans and covered them with crumpled-up newsprint so the boss wouldn't see - the boss being Taylor. After they spent about an hour sipping beer on the sneak, Taylor got up from his desk in the far corner of the room and walked slowly toward the wastebasket where the beer was hiding. Everyone froze, but no one said a word. Upon reaching his destination, Taylor stopped, reached through the waste paper, grabbed a beer, shook the excess water off the can and walked it slowly back to his office. The sports guys, who had visions of being out on the street and out of a job, just sat there speechless.

I will always have a warm sport in my heart for Taylor, who was a great investigative reporter before becoming a Pulitzer-Prize winning editor. He gave me my first political reporting job and remained a constant booster, even after I left the Utica newspapers for a stint in Albany. After his retirement, he became an unpaid adviser to Mayor Hanna. He never lost his love of and respect for politics and politicians.

A Men's Room Job Interview

I got my first taste of state politics in Albany, the New York state capital, in the Spring of 1976. While still a reporter at the Utica newspapers, I drove 90 miles east on the Thruway to attend the New York State Legislative Correspondents Association annual dinner and lampoon show. It was and remains a black-tie affair attended by state legislators, their staffs, lobbyists, business and news executives, mayors from around the state and even the governor himself. Usually held toward the end of the spring legislative session, the LCA show is the social highlight of the Albany political year. I didn't know that at the time. But I quickly found out. And it set the stage for the next chapter in my reporting career.

It all began one March afternoon when Gil Smith, the new executive editor of the Utica newspapers, called me into his glass-enclosed office in the far corner of the newsroom. "What does he want?" I asked myself. A summons to the Smith office usually meant one of two things: You did something wrong and were about to be admonished, or he had some particularly unpalatable assignment for you that required his authority to enforce. So I got up from my desk with some trepidation. Smith was a dapper man. He always wore crisp white shirts and silk ties. He had slick, thinning black hair and a pencil moustache. When you glanced up at him in his fishbowl office, he always seemed to be either meeting with his managing and city editors, Tony Vella and Frank Tomaino, or talking on the phone. As I made my way past the clutter of reporters' desks, I noticed he was on the phone. Glancing up, he saw me hesitate, but waved me in. When I walked through the door he was saying goodbye to his caller and motioned me to sit down. "What is this all about?" I wondered.

Smith, a stern taskmaster, but an eminently fair boss, leaned forward and said with a slight smirk, "How would you like to take a trip to Albany?"

I immediately figured he wanted me to go there to cover some story. Earlier that year I had gone down to the Governor's Mansion where Gov. Hugh Carey had held a briefing for state newspaper reporters on his annual budget. "What's happening in Albany?" I asked.

"Well," he said. "Every year the Albany reporters put on a little dinner and show and they invite editors from papers around the state to attend. Neither Tony, Frank nor I can make it, so we thought you might like to go."

I didn't hesitate one second. "Sure," I responded, flattered that they would ask me to go in their place. "When is it?"

"Next month. April 4, a Saturday," he replied. "You drive down. We'll pay for your hotel and your tuxedo rental and reimburse you for your mileage," he said. "I'll call the *Gannett News Service* bureau in Albany and tell them to put you down."

"Wow!" I thought. This is a big deal. The trip could cost $150, a lot of money at that time. Gannett, the parent company of the Utica newspapers, had a news bureau in Albany. Its four reporters covered state government and politics for the Gannett-owned newspapers around the state, which at that time included, in addition to Utica, daily publications in Niagara Falls, Rochester, Elmira, Binghamton, Ithaca, Saratoga Springs, Poughkeepsie, Yonkers and a group of suburban newspapers in Westchester and Rockland Counties. All in all, they took in a good part of the state. I was excited. The by-lines of the Gannett reporters in Albany were familiar to me. The Utica newspapers often ran their dispatches from the state capital. In my eyes, they were big-time journalists, and I was going to hobnob with them. Terrific!

When the big day came, my wife Carol and I drove to Albany and checked in at the Thruway Motel, where the dinner and show were being held. A reservation had been made in my name. The clerk handed me an envelope. In it was the dinner ticket and an invitation to a pre-dinner reception being hosted by Gannett. The hotel was abuzz with people coming in for the dinner and I felt my excitement mount as I removed my tuxedo from its plastic bag. Women weren't allowed at the LCA dinner in those "enlightened" days of 1976 (they are now) so my wife stayed in the room until the post-dinner reception, where she joined me.

Not wanting to be the first one to walk into the reception, I waited until 6:45 before I made my entrance. But I was dressed by 6 and spent the next 45 minutes pacing the room, trying not to sit down, worried that I would wrinkle the sharply pressed black tuxedo trousers. The reception room, one of those nondescript hotel function rooms we've all been in -

you know, the ones with names like the Rensselaer Room or the Schuyler Room - was already filled with tuxedo-clad men holding cocktail glasses and chattering. At first glance, I didn't know anyone there and felt uncomfortable. I walked over to the bar and got a drink - ginger ale. I wasn't much of a drinker and I figured that was safe. One fellow, seeing me standing there looking a little lost came up and introduced himself. He was Ralph Soda, managing editor of *The Saratogian*, then a Gannett newspaper in Saratoga Springs. We hit it off right away. Perhaps it was because we were both Italian-American. But over the years we developed a deep personal friendship, working together on several investigative projects in Albany and later in Washington, D.C. One of our probes into the odd spending practices of the New York State Legislature won an *Associated Press* reporting prize in 1979. He went on to win the prestigious Worth Bingham Award in 1980 for his unearthing of the Hunt brothers scam that artificially sent silver prices soaring. Before he died in 2004 he made me promise him that I would finish this book.

At the reception, which was attended by a number of state legislators who I recognized and a lot of people who looked very important, I was introduced to John Curley, who was then the managing editor of the *Gannett News Service* in Washington, D.C. Curley, who later went on to be come chairman and CEO of Gannett Co. Inc., was a tall, easy-going fellow with a quick smile who I guessed to be not too much older than me, perhaps in his late 30s. He brought me over to the bar to get a drink and seemed to be familiar with some of the work I was doing at the Utica newspapers. I was flattered. He also introduced me to several other Gannett editors from Washington and from newspapers around the state, names I knew and heard, but had never attached to real people. Everyone was friendly and welcoming. And many proved to be pretty good drinkers, too, judging from how they seemed to grow more jovial as the evening went on.

One political celebrity I met at the reception was U.S. Sen. James Buckley, of New York, the crew-cut brother of conservative commentator William F. Buckley Jr. The senator was running for re-election on the Conservative Party line, so he figured attendance at this Albany gathering of the state's top news people was a political must. It didn't help, however. Buckley was defeated that November by Democrat Daniel P. Moynihan, who went on to serve four distinguished terms in the U.S. Senate before retiring in 2001.

At the dinner, held in the hotel's large ballroom, I sat next to Curley, the apparent leader of the tuxedoed, all-male contingent from Gannett, which numbered about 20. He casually ordered, with the wave of an arm, several bottles of wine for his Gannett charges. Before the main course arrived, the bottles were empty, triggering a murmur for more. Curley got the message and ordered another round.

After dinner, the stage lit up and a five-piece band that sounded like something you would hear at an Italian wedding began playing. The members of the Albany press corps put on their show, which in story and song made fun of the state's politicians, from the governor on down. Judging from the guffaws their slapstick antics elicited from the savvy crowd, the show was a hit. I don't remember what the joke was, but John Omicinski of the *Gannett News Service,* who was to become my Albany colleague and close friend, played Buckley in a basketball uniform, bouncing the ball erratically as he sang, "Senator Buckleee...." to the tune of the Beatles' "Eleanor Rigby." The tagline was, "All the Senate hopefuls, where do they all come from? All the Senate hopefuls, why do they all go wrong?"

The *New York Daily News'* inimitable Tom Poster, in a long blond wig and slinky satin gown, his face comically smudged with red rouge, red lipstick and purple eye shadow, pranced and bumped his ample hips across the stage to the brassy tune of "Lulu's Back in Town." A "Lulu" in Albany parlance, is the taxpayer-hated extra stipend or other perk a state legislator gets in addition to his or her pay.

It was that kind of a show. I loved it. The politicians in the crowd seemed to love it, too. I found out later that politicians would rather be the butt of jokes in the show than ignored. They wore their inclusion like badges of honor, no matter how sharply they were skewered. And some were sharply skewered.

There was nothing subtle about the jokes. Much of the comedy was strictly vaudeville. In 1977, in a "Wizard of Oz" sketch, Mary Anne Kruspak, then New York's lieutenant governor, was depicted as the scarecrow in search of a brain. In 1980, when then-New York congressman Jack Kemp, the former Buffalo Bills quarterback, backed out of challenging U.S. Sen. Jacob Javits in a Republican primary, his timidity was lambasted by a reporter wearing a chicken outfit and a football helmet. The song was "Y.M.C.A." I don't remember the lyrics, but I think of

Kemp whenever I hear that song.

During the intermission, I got up to go to the men's room. Standing at the urinal, I glanced over and saw Curley standing in the stall next to me. He turned and asked me if I liked the show. I said I did. He then asked me if I had ever thought about working in Albany. I said I hadn't, but I offered something lame like, "I think it might be interesting." Little did I know at the time that Curley, the future CEO of Gannett, was conducting a job interview from a urinal stall. I am not making this up.

About a week later, Smith called me into his office again.

"The *Gannett News Service* Albany bureau needs some help covering the end of the legislative session. Do you think you could go down for two weeks and help out?" he asked.

"Sure," I replied, "as long as its alright with you."

"It's not alright with me," he said with a wry smile. "Damn it! I don't want to lose you. I think they want you to go to work in Albany and are giving you a tryout. I won't stand in your way. If that's what you want, go ahead. It would be a good career move."

I didn't know what to say. I wasn't looking to leave Utica. It was my home town and we had settled in nicely there. My wife and I had bought our first home a year earlier, which we liked very much, and our daughter Kristen was in 4th grade with a lot of friends. A move to Albany would be jarring for all. A house would have to be sold, another one bought. My wife, a teacher, would have to find a new job. It was overwhelming. But I told Smith I would try the two-week stint in Albany, figuring that would at least buy me a little time to decide what to do. Maybe I wouldn't like it.

So early on a Monday in mid-May, I packed my suitcase and drove to Albany, where I checked in at the Howard Johnson motel. Shag carpet was big at that time and my room had an orange one. It would be my home for the next two weeks. After dropping off my bag, I drove downtown and parked my car in the garage beneath the gigantic, ultra-modern government complex of marble, glass and steel built by Nelson Rockefeller - notoriously known as "The Mall" - and walked though the tunnel that linked it to the State Capitol, where the *Gannett News Service* office was located. I generously use the word "office." It was really a cubby hole tucked into the rear of a balcony - dubbed by insiders as "The Shelf" - in the Press Room on the third floor of the Capitol between the Senate and Assembly chambers. Besides accommodating the *Gannett News Service*,

The Shelf also served as home for Albany reporters for *Newsday*, the *New York Times*, and the *Buffalo Evening News*. The front of The Shelf, which was a mezzanine that overlooked the main floor of the press room, featured a piano, which bore a plaque that said it was once played by Harry Truman, a beat up poker table and a green-covered, full-size pool table.

The poker table was seldom empty, no matter what time of day. One of its main denizens was Victor Ostrowidzki, of the *Albany Times Union*, who seemed to have a permanent chair there. If he wasn't embroiled in a game, he would sit alone and play solitaire. One evening, when a hot budget battle was raging between the governor and the legislature, Victor, waiting for the next break in the fight to occur, was elbows deep in a heavy poker game. Warren Anderson, the Republican Senate majority leader from Binghamton, walked onto the main floor of the press room and began to provide reporters with an update. With all of us up against deadlines, we crowded around Anderson and fired questions at him. An urgent voice called down from The Shelf, "Warren! Warren!" Anderson looked up and there was Victor peeking over the railing with his cards fanned out in his hand. "What are they going to do about the funds for the Albany Sewage Treatment Plant? he asked. Anderson, who was hardly astonished at the interruption from above, paused and shouted up an answer. Obviously satisfied with what he heard, Victor disappeared and went back to his game.

Every afternoon at 5 p.m., a crackly old oil cloth would be spread over the press room pool table and bottles of whiskey, gin and beer would be placed there for the daily happy hour, which was enjoyed by one and all. The liquid refreshments were generously provided courtesy of the New York State Automobile Dealers Association and other lobbying groups. In the mid-70s, few journalists worried about the ethical proprieties of the press accepting free booze from the folks they covered. In those days, many reporters believed that Freedom of the Press meant everything for the press was free. But the post-Watergate push for ethics was starting to take hold. The year I got there, not only did they reform the Legislative Correspondents Association by allowing women to come to the dinner, they also stopped accepting free liquor, or free anything else, from the lobbying groups. And that included perks like free passes to state-owned ski areas such as Gore and Whiteface Mountains, and tickets to shows and sporting events. Albany veterans were appalled. These new young kids and women, they said, were ruining everything.

My first assignment during my Albany tryout was to attend hearings of the New York State Public Service Commission, which was being petitioned by the Rochester Gas and Electric Company, Niagara Mohawk Power Corporation and the Power Authority of the State of New York for permits to build two giant 765-kilovolt transmission lines that would carry hydro-generated electrical power from Canada to energy-starved New York City and other parts of the state. The hearings had been going on for about seven months and were dragging on because there was a lot of public objection over the potential health risks and environmental hazards the siting of such lines might present. I didn't know anything about the controversy and tried to bone up as fast as I could. But when I got to the hearing room in one of those glass-steel-and-marble skyscrapers on The Mall, I was quickly overwhelmed by the technical detail witnesses were presenting.

Scientists testified and presented papers on the deaths of rats exposed to the electromagnetic fields generated by such lines, and projected that they could kill cows grazing under the wires and worse, cause cancer in humans working or living near them.. Environmentalists complained about how unsightly the massive steel-framed towers that would carry the lines would look on the Upstate New York landscape, especially as they made their way through the scenic Adirondack and Catskill Mountains. Supporters, mainly the power companies and industries saying they could save money on the cost of electricity if the lines were built, told frightening stories about how the coming energy shortage could lead to serious blackouts and extended shutdowns of commerce all across the state.

My job was to attend two or three days of hearings and write a summary story outlining the problem, giving the arguments of both sides and projecting what might be coming next. After sitting in that hearing room for about an hour listening to lawyers drone on about some technicality, I quickly got the sneaking suspicion that this was one of those stories with no conclusion that none of the regular reporters in the bureau wanted to do. It had probably been requested by one or more of the Gannett newspapers around the state, but had been pushed to the back burner just waiting for some rube like me to come along and put it back on the heat.

The hearings dragged on for another year. After I joined the bureau,

I became the 765-kv guy. I would occasionally attend the hearings and file wire stories on their progress. Finally, approval was granted and the lines were built in the early 1980s. Now, nearly a quarter century later, in the aftermath of the August 2003 Northeast blackout, New York is hearing new arguments for the building of new power plants and more transmission lines. It goes to show that the news is a continuing cycle. It never ends. Hang around long enough and the story you covered decades ago pops up again and again in slightly different form.

One story I covered in my Albany days that still keeps coming back is the battle over what to do about PCBs in the upper Hudson River. When I was in Albany, the controversy was still unfolding and I wrote some stories that helped bring it to light. Starting in the early 1950s, two General Electric plants in Fort Edward and Hudson Falls, N.Y. began using PCBs - polychlorinated biphenyls - in the manufacture of electrical capacitors and discharging the chemicals into the Hudson River, which was adjacent to the factories By the early 1970s, serious questions were being raised about the toxic effects on humans who ate fish contaminated by the PCBs in the water. By the mid-1970s, with the health hazards becoming more publicized and fish in the Hudson showing more contamination, GE stopped using PCBs. But a pitched battle began over what to do with the up to 1.3 million tons of PCB sediments found in various concentrations along a 200-mile stretch of the Hudson from Hudson Falls, about 50 miles north of Albany, to the tip of Manhattan Island, about 150 miles south, and who would pay for the cleanup. Twenty-nine years after I first began writing about the problem, plans are still being finalized on how the contaminated sediments can be dredged and buried safely.

During my Albany tryout, I got my first taste of what it was like to cover a legislative session as bills were being debated and voted upon on the Senate and Assembly floors. Walking into the New York State Senate chamber for the first time, I was overwhelmed by its magnificence, so red and so regal. Red carpeting covered the floor. Hand-carved red Caribbean mahogany wainscoting on the walls was set off by panels of hand-tooled red leather. The chamber's soaring columns were carved from Italian red marble. The senators sat on high-backed, red leather-upholstered chairs behind antique mahogany slant-topped desks, arrayed in a horseshoe pattern beneath ornate brass chandeliers that hung from long chains anchored in the gold-leaf-trimmed, carved ceiling high above. The reporters' seats, wooden chairs with arms for writing on, like the kind you find in college classrooms, only nicer, were down on the Senate floor, their backs up against the mahogany podium where the lieutenant governor presided. Senators at the ends of the first row were close enough for reporters to reach out and touch.

One of those senators so close I could hear her and her adjacent colleagues chattering among themselves was Carol Bellamy, a Democrat from Manhattan. She was more recently executive director of UNICEF, and heard often on TV and radio discussing efforts to aid victims of the day-after-Christmas 2004 earthquake and tsunami that devastated islands in the Indian Ocean and killed more than 150,000 people. Ballamy, after leaving the New York Senate, was elected the first woman president of the New York City Council. She later ran unsuccessfully on the Liberal Party line for mayor of New York City. She was defeated in 1985 by Democratic incumbent Ed Koch, with whom she repeatedly clashed. Speaking of Koch to the *New York Times* that year, she memorably said, "I think he is an entertainer. I would prefer if he were a performer."

Koch, of course, was and still is an entertainer - a politician always full of himself. To the rest of America, he was the quintessential New Yorker - irreverent, brash, quick with a quip, slow to listen and remarkably ignorant of what the world was like west of the Hudson River, north of the Bronx, east of Queens and south of Brooklyn. He found that out the hard way when he ran for New York governor in 1982 and lost the Democratic primary to underdog Mario Cuomo, who successfully painted Koch as out of touch with Upstate New York's people and problems. In an interview with *Playboy* magazine, Koch alienated upstaters by referring to life in the suburbs as "sterile," and worse, "wasting time in a pickup truck when you have to drive 20 miles to buy a gingham dress or a Sears, Roebuck suit." When he was defeated, he dismissed it by saying he didn't really want to be governor anyway.

But Koch viewed himself as bigger than life, and never suffered fools gladly. When he was angry with you, he let you know. I experienced the Koch wrath first hand on Labor Day 1980 when I was in Queens covering New York's Democratic primary for the U.S. Senate. The candidate I was following that day was Bess Myerson, the tall, dark-haired former Miss America, New York consumer advocate and frequent TV game-show

54   *A Men's Room Job Interview*

panelist in the 1950s and 60s. Myerson, at the time, was a close friend of
Koch and his frequent date. Many wondered if marriage was in the future.
That day, Myerson had the mayor with her as she campaigned among
the membership of the mostly Jewish beach clubs of Queens. The beach
clubs were anything but what their name implied. They were private,
fenced, concrete-paved enclaves in the middle of the city where heavily
tanned women in big sunglasses sat under umbrella tables by a swimming
pool, which hardly anyone used, playing mahjong and canasta. Their
husbands, sitting around tables farther back, played poker, smoked cigars
and listened to the Yankees or Mets games on transistor radios.

Myerson was running against two other big-name women politicians:
Rep. Elizabeth Holtzman, of Brooklyn, who won national attention for
her tough questioning of witnesses six years earlier as a member of the
House Judiciary Committee looking into the Watergate scandal that
eventually toppled Richard Nixon, and Rep. Bella Abzug, she of the big
hats and the big presence, known far and wide for her rough-and-tumble
battles on behalf of women's rights and against the Vietnam War.

Also in that race trying to make a political comeback was former
New York mayor John Lindsay. But Lindsay's political star had long faded
and he ran pretty much in the shadow of the three women in the primary.
I remember him walking through the park near the State Capitol in Albany
shortly before the primary and shaking hands with state workers. He had
only one or two reporters and no cameras following him. His presence
hardly evoked a yawn. Back in the days when he was New York City's
matinee-idol mayor, he moved like a queen bee with a media swarm
constantly buzzing around him. It was a sad reminder of how quickly
defeated politicians lose not only their luminous aura, but also their public
attention. No one, it seems, likes a loser, no matter how much he or she
was liked when they were winning. We use up politicians like paper cups.

On the day I was covering Myerson, I asked her press secretary if I
might get a few minutes for an interview sometime during the afternoon.
It was decided she would do it in her car while riding between stops. That
sounded fine to me. Reporters often conduct interviews on the fly, rather
than sit down in some formal setting like an office and hold a long
conversation. I have interviewed candidates not only while riding in cars,
but also in airplanes, on trains, while walking - sometimes running - down
busy streets, in restaurants, backstage before or after a speech, sitting on

a park bench. You do it wherever and whenever you can.

On this day I got into the back seat of Koch's mayoral limousine with Myerson. Koch got in the front seat and immediately turned around, put his arms on the seat back and peered at us. When I asked Myerson my first question, Koch quickly answered. When I asked my second question, he answered again. On the third, Myerson began to answer and Koch cut in. At that point, I was starting to panic. I only had a few minutes for the interview and I wasn't getting anything from Myerson. So I made the decision, with trepidation, to ask Koch politely if he would let Myerson answer the questions. As I expected, Koch blew up. "You are my guest in my car! Do you want to get out right here and walk?" he asked. "No sir," I answered. "But I would like to get this interview with Miss Myerson."

Koch spun around in a snit. He never said a word during the rest of the interview. I was lucky I didn't get thrown out of the car in the middle of Queens. It was a long way back to Manhattan. But at the next stop, he was his old jovial self and acted is if the incident never happened.

On occasion, I have conducted interviews in the homes of politicians. Often, they are the best ones. Politicians seem to let their guards down in the friendly confines of their homes and reveal things they might not if they are sitting behind a desk or in a broadcast studio. My first at-home interview was with Michael Caruso, who was running for mayor of Utica in 1971. I remember it well not for what he had to say, but for the cordial hospitality of his late wife Sandy, who brought me coffee and delicate Italian pastries before I could even get started. I don't recall if I ate any of the pastries, but I do remember how kind she was. She never lost her kindness when she became the city's first lady, always smiling, always polite, always very gentle and always a lady in the traditional sense. She remained active in Republican politics long after her husband dropped out, going on to become Oneida County clerk. Sandy died of cancer in 2000, while still in office.

Seven years later, another political wife, Matilda Cuomo, whose husband Mario was running for New York lieutenant governor, served me a family delicacy, steamed heads of escarole, their green leaves stuffed with Fontina cheese and breadcrumbs. Those I did eat, with gusto, as did Mario Cuomo, who had just returned to his Queens home after a long day of campaigning. It was apparently a tradition that Matilda had something to eat waiting for her husband when he returned, no matter how late he got in. Cuomo, who went on to win three terms as governor of the Empire State, was a funny guy. He abhorred staying in hotels and would often travel hundreds of miles just to get home and sleep in his own bed. Once, when I asked him why he decided not to run for president, he said, candidly, "They told me that if I ran, I would have to spend 90 days in Iowa. I don't want to spend 90 days in Iowa."

I got the job in Albany and figured I had hit the big time. Not only would I be writing for the Utica newspapers, I also would have my byline appearing in more than a dozen other papers around the state. And don't let reporters who have been around a while kid you when they say bylines mean nothing to them. Seeing your byline in print is like looking in the mirror every day to assure yourself that you are still alive. It's a daily fix. And if you go too many days without it, panic sets in.

"This Isn't the
Yankees' Dressing Room!"

I started working in Albany in September 1976, in time to cover the fall running of New York's U.S. Senate race. It featured Democrat Daniel Patrick Moynihan, the former ambassador to India, United Nations ambassador, former aide in the Nixon White House and distinguished scholar, and the incumbent, James Buckley. Buckley, a successful New York lawyer and brother of conservative commentator William F. Buckley Jr., won a three-way Senate race six years earlier on the Conservative Party line, beating Dick Ottinger, then a Democratic congressman from Westchester County, and Republican Charles Goodell, who was appointed to the seat in 1968 by New York Gov. Nelson Rockefeller following the assassination of Robert Kennedy. At the time of his appointment, Goodell was an up-and-coming Republican congressman representing a largely rural, conservative district in Western New York centered in Jamestown. But when he was named Kennedy's successor, he overnight became a liberal, angering many Republicans in the state. President Nixon, miffed at Goodell's voting with Democrats in the Senate on key issues and his outspoken criticism of the Vietnam War, unleashed his attack dog, Vice President Spiro Agnew. Nixon sent Agnew out to help Buckley and defeat the man who he saw as a turncoat. Agnew did his part, calling Goodell "The Christine Jorgensen of the Republican Party." Jorgensen, in the 1950s, was the first man to successfully undergo a sex-change operation. The remark drew heavy media attention, and helped highlight, in shorthand, the case being made against Goodell.

I was assigned to cover Moynihan. I followed him on the campaign trail, mostly in the New York City area, where the bulk of the Democratic vote was concentrated. But what I remember most was that at night, after the last speech was given, Moynihan, his staff and the reporters covering him would together head for a nearby bar, sit down and have few beers. In those days, rules were different. We all automatically assumed that once we sat down in a less-formal setting, everything was off the record, or at least on deep background, which meant whatever you learned could not directly be attributed to its source. While I was one of the younger reporters out there, most of my colleagues were veterans on the New York political scene - respected reporters such as Frank Lynn and Maurice Carroll of the *New York Times*, Eugene Spagnoli of the *New York Daily News*, Arthur Greenspan of the *New York Post*, Bill Stevens of *UPI* and Dick Zander and Al Eisen of *Newsday*. They weren't out to get anyone. They were out to report the story of the campaign. If during one of those evening social sessions someone told an off-color joke or made a nasty remark about his opponent, no one ran to report it. We knew that once the pencils and pads were put away, the ground rules changed.

Not any more. Now, everything is fair game. If reporters hear a candidate say something, they feel free to report it, regardless of whether it was said in private or public. As a result, candidates and office holders have become more guarded, limiting their exposure to reporters to formal, often-tightly-scripted sessions, making it difficult for the media to give the public a more-complete picture of what the person seeking their vote is really like. Seeing politicians in private situations where they feel free to be themselves tells a lot more about their character, personality and sincerity than more-formal, arms-length encounters on the campaign trail can ever pick up.

What I learned about Moynihan, beside the fact that he enjoyed a glass of beer, was that he could be very funny, very engaging and not such a big shot that he had no interest in you. He took time to find out who I was, where I came from, where I went to college. It turned out that he once taught at my alma mater, Syracuse University, which quickly gave us a friendly reference point. While he was a great intellectual who was far smarter than any of the scribes sitting around his table, he never lectured or tried to make you feel dumb. He listened to your thoughts, discussed them and respected them. And he was courteous to a fault, standing when women walked over to his table, often bowing in greeting. I don't remember any off-color jokes Moynihan might have told, but I do remember that when we sat around those saloon tables, we all laughed a lot. And nobody went out the next day and pulled his punches on the guy they were covering. Calling them as we saw them was the thread that ran though all of our coverage. Politicians didn't want favors from reporters, they wanted fairness.

In 1978, while covering Mario Cuomo's campaign for lieutenant governor, I marched along with him in Utica's Columbus Day parade, the social highlight of the year for Italian-Americans. It was an unusual summer-like day for mid-October. After the parade, he made an appearance in nearby Rome, where his audience again was mostly Italian-Americans. At that time he was not that well known around the state. He had been a largely obscure secretary of state, appointed to the post by Gov. Hugh Carey in 1975. But Carey had tapped him to be his running mate in 1978 after the incumbent lieutenant governor, Mary Anne Krupsak, challenged Carey in a primary and lost. Cuomo used his Italian-American heritage to good advantage in New York's upstate cities, which had large Italian-American populations, swelled by the many Italian immigrants who flocked there in the early 1900s to work in factories and on railroads strung from Albany to Buffalo along the old Erie Canal. I recall Cuomo drawing a big laugh from his Rome audience when he joked, "My wife Matilda is Sicilian. Do you know what it's like to sleep with a woman who keeps a knife in her nylons?"

After the Rome appearance, Cuomo had one more stop for the day. He had to go back to Utica, about 15 miles, to speak at a labor union dinner. On the way, he stopped at a motel to freshen up. The only reporter traveling with him, I was invited into the motel room to wait while he changed his clothes. (Imagine politicians feeling comfortable enough to let a reporter do that now.) Cuomo had a clean shirt with him, but he had no extra suit. And his suit, after being worn all day in the 80-degree heat, was looking pretty rumpled. One aide suggested that he take the wrinkles out of his pants by steaming them in the shower. So Cuomo took off his pants, hung them in the shower, turned the hot water on and sat down on the bed in his undershorts and socks. We continued to talk politics as the shower ran and steam wafted out from under the closed bathroom door.

Suddenly, the phone rang. Cuomo answered. It was the motel manager calling to say there was a reporter from the *Oneida Dispatch* who had come to interview him. "Send him down," Cuomo said. Within a minute, there was a knock on the door. Cuomo, still in his shorts, walked over, opened the door and then quickly slammed it shut.

"It's a woman!" he gasped, turning to us with a Charlie Brown grin on his face. Turning back, he opened the door a crack and said to the puzzled young woman, "I'm sorry. I'm not dressed. I'll be with you in a minute. This isn't the Yankees dressing room, you know." We all roared. It was a reference to the controversy then going on over whether women sportswriters should be allowed in the New York Yankees dressing room. They eventually got in, although many of the players continued to walk around naked.

But not Cuomo. He ran into the bathroom, turned off the shower and quickly put on his pants. Scurrying back out, he ran to the door and let the woman reporter in. It was hard to determine who was more embarrassed, she or Cuomo. But she got her interview. And Cuomo got his publicity, even after being caught with his pants down.

Ironically, the next day, Cuomo was in Manhattan where he and other political dignitaries participated in the ticker-tape parade up Broadway for the 1978 World Series Champion Yankees. That was the series where the Bronx Bombers beat the Los Angeles Dodgers, four games to one. It will long be remembered as the series highlighted by Reggie Jackson's record three home runs in the fifth and final game. A lifelong Yankee fan myself - in the Italian-American neighborhood where I grew up, Joe DiMaggio was not just a hero, he was a god - I was thrilled to be going to the parade. Cuomo rode in a car with his running mate, Gov. Hugh Carey. I rode in the parade on a press truck, its flat bed jammed with reporters and cameras. With the cheers of the crowd ringing in our ears and the ticker tape and confetti cascading over us like feathery snow, I felt like a hero myself. And for one fleeting moment, I got a taste of what it was like to be what nearly every boy I knew wanted to be when he grew up - a New York Yankee.

Carey, the New York governor I covered during my Albany years, was one of those rare politicians who was not big on attending sports events. He didn't like risking the boos that inevitably come when politicians are introduced to the fans. He rarely showed up at World Series games in New York, although he was a baseball fan, a loyal son of Brooklyn and devoted follower of the Dodgers. He wasn't a fixture at New York Knicks basketball games, either, although those were the days when the Knicks legends Bill Bradley, who went on to become a U.S. senator from New Jersey, Willis Reed, Walt Frazier, Dave DeBusschere and Earl "The Pearl" Monroe strode the Madison Square Garden hardwoods.

But sports fan or not, everyone figured Carey would show up at the 1980 Winter Olympics being held at Lake Placid, N.Y. Those were the

"Miracle on Ice" Olympics, when the young and inexperienced United States hockey team did the impossible. They beat the mighty Soviets Army team, 4-3, and went on to win the Gold Medal. Carey was the governor of the host state. Surely he would attend. Franklin D. Roosevelt, who was New York governor when the Olympics were held in Lake Placid in 1932, was a prominent participant in the opening of those games. It was that same year that Roosevelt went on to win the presidency. But Carey, 38 years later, did not go.

He refused to attend because he was angered by news reports critical of his plan to spend some $250,000 in state funds to winterize a state-owned Adirondack Great Camp, Topridge, on nearby Saranac Lake, willed to the State by Post cereal heir and socialite Marjorie Meriweather Post. Carey wanted to spruce the place up so he could host visiting foreign dignitaries and heads of state coming in for the Olympics. The news reports cast the expenditure as a reckless extravagance, picturing Carey throwing lavish parties at taxpayer expense. Carey, who had a bit of a thin skin and was quick to anger at personal criticism, cancelled his plans to host parties and never showed up at the Olympics. He sent Mario Cuomo, his lieutenant governor, to participate in the opening ceremonies in his place. Carey was that kind of guy - a most unusual politician who rarely sought the limelight, and sometimes stubborn to a fault, often spiting himself to make a point or stick to a principle.

Oddly enough, the president of the United States at the time, Jimmy Carter, didn't show up at those Olympics, either. Carter was in the middle of dealing with the Iranian hostage crisis and facing a tough Democratic presidential primary challenge from Massachusetts Sen. Edward Kennedy. He figured going to the Olympics would look too frivolous. Besides, he was calling for a U.S. boycott of the 1980 Summer Games to be held in Moscow as a protest against the 1979 Soviet invasion of Afghanistan. So he couldn't very well show up at the Winter Games, in the U.S, which the Soviets were participating in, without looking to be somewhat of a hypocrite. He sent his vice president, Walter Mondale to do the opening honors. Few Americans realized then, or realize now, that neither the president of the host country nor the governor of the host state attended the Lake Placid games. That would be akin to President George W. Bush and Utah Gov. Mike Leavitt not showing up at the 2002 Salt Lake City Winter Games, or President Bill Clinton and Georgia Gov. Zell Miller not attending the Atlanta Summer Games in 1996. They all did.

What made the Lake Placid absence of Carey and Carter all the more ironic was the astonishing feat of the U.S. hockey team, which created arguably the most memorable single moment for Americans of any Olympics held in recent decades. I was lucky enough to attend that game. As a reporter for the *Gannett News Service* based in Albany, N.Y. in the late 70s, the assignment of covering the plans for the games to be held in nearby Lake Placid fell to me. The State of New York put millions into their staging. Besides, it was a story of nationwide interest. So from time to time, over a period of three years, I would travel north to that Adirondack resort village and report on the progress of the construction of the various venues such as the ski jumps and the ice arena, the logistics of housing, feeding and transporting the thousands of athletes, workers, tourists and media representatives who would make their way to the big event and the battle between the planners and environmentalists over whether all the new construction was damaging the natural beauty of the area. Construction of the ski jump, condemned as an eyesore on the scenic landscape, was held up for months by environmental protests and lawsuits.

So when in late 1979 the *Gannett News Service* put together a team of reporters to cover the Olympics themselves, I was made part of the squad, a serious and sober government reporter among a gang of Good-Time-Charlie sportswriters. I never had so much fun. My assignment was to continue reporting on the things I had been reporting on - how were the plans working in reality and anything else beside the sports events that might be interesting to readers. As it turned out, the elaborate plan that would close the Olympic zone to most vehicular traffic and rely on shuttle buses to carry everyone back and forth from their hotels to the sporting-event sites was a disaster. For whatever reason, the planners woefully underestimated the number of buses needed for the task. The result was that over the first few days, people were stuck for hours in near-zero temperatures waiting for buses to show up. And naturally, when reporters are inconvenienced, they are going to use the great stage they have to tell the world about it. Therefore, the first news reports out of the 1980 Lake Placid Olympics were not about skiers and skaters, jumpers and bobsledders. They were about how the bus plan wasn't working. TV cameras filmed the clusters of chilled Olympic revelers, the steam of their breath fogging the air, waiting for buses that never came. The pictures were beamed around the world from Singapore to Helsinki.

The lines for the buses were so long after the Opening Ceremonies of the games that many people decided to walk four miles back to the village. The clusters of trekkers on the highway were so thick that the few buses that there were had to honk and honk their horns to get the pedestrians to move out of the way. And as they passed, the walkers booed, shouted catcalls and shook their fists. I walked back with legendary sportswriter Red Smith, then with the *New York Times* and still writing in his late 70s. Smith will long be remembered for once saying, "Writing is easy. You just cut open a vein and bleed." I worried about Smith walking that distance, but he gruffly insisted that he was fine. When we got back, he was a little short of breath and his cheeks were quite rosy. But he immediately sat down at his typewriter in the press center, which was in the Lake Placid High School, and started writing. As we walked, he told me stories, at my prodding, about his coverage of some of the most historic sports events of the 20th Century - Jackie Robinson breaking baseball's color line in 1947, Don Larson's perfect game in the 1956 World Series, the New York Giants-Baltimore Colts NFL Championship Game in 1958 and the Cassius Clay-Sonny Liston fight in 1962 .

But little did we know that in a few days, the plucky U.S. hockey team would create another of those milestones in Smith's long and glorious career by shocking the world and beating a far-more-experienced-and-skilled Soviet team. When the game was over and mayhem broke out down on the ice, I ran out of the arena and immediately called our editing desk back in Washington, D.C. to ask if they needed any color reports, in addition to the accounts of the game itself, which others were writing. My editor, Jerry Langdon, told me to go out on the streets and report the scene. So I ran outside into the cold night air and saw immediately that the celebration was already well under way. Horns were honking, flags were waving, crowds were cheering and searchlights that had been set up to give dramatic effect to the nightly Olympic telecasts on ABC were waving across the sky. Adding to the picture, a light snow had begun to fall. I pushed my way into the crowd, stopped people and asked them how they were feeling, scribbled it into my notebook and moved on. After about 15 minutes of observations and quickly snatched interviews, I ran to a public phone - there were no cell phones then - and called in my story , dictating without writing, since time was short. It went something like this:

"LAKE PLACID, N.Y. - It was New Years Eve in Times Square in this snowy Olympic village Friday night as cheering crowds of jubilant Americans waved the Stars and Stripes, honked their horns, hugged, kissed and cheered until they were hoarse in celebration of the U.S. hockey team's incredible 4-3 defeat of the mighty Soviets in a game that will be remembered long after we are gone."

The story went out over the *Gannett News Service* wire, serving Gannett Company's then nearly 90 newspapers across the country. It ran on many front pages the next morning under my byline. Seeing those clips later was a thrill I will never forget. I would have never got the story if Mike Shostak, a sports reporter for the *Providence Journal*, hadn't found a ticket and given it to me. Pure luck, which is the way some of the best scoops and opportunities in the news business often turn up.

When I got to Albany, one of the beats I was assigned was education. That meant covering the New York State Board of Regents, the governing body for the state's elementary and secondary schools, and the State University of New York Board of Trustees, overseer of the state's then 64 state-supported community colleges, colleges and universities.

In 1976, my rookie year in the state capital, Ernest Boyer, a soft-spoken, gray-haired Quaker, was the SUNY chancellor, the top gun of the state college system. But before I got to know him very well, he was on his way out. In early 1977, newly elected President Jimmy Carter named Boyer to be U.S. commissioner of Education. In those days, there was no secretary of Education. So small was the federal government's involvement in education, then still considered primarily a local responsibility, that it had not yet been elevated to Cabinet level. There was a federal Office of Education in Washington and Boyer had been chosen to run it. But before he left Albany, I made an appointment to interview him to get his take on the job he did in New York and some thoughts about what he saw as the challenges facing him in Washington.

The only appointment I could get with Boyer was on his final night in town. I drove over to his state-owned house, a sprawling brick two-story colonial on one of Albany's nicest residential streets. It was raining as, notebook in hand, I ran past an orange-and-white U-Haul truck backed into the driveway and up to the front door . I rang the bell and in a few seconds Boyer himself, in a black sweatshirt and jeans, opened the door and welcomed me in. As I made my way across the parquet-floored foyer,

I could see cardboard boxes piled all around. Boyer told me he had begun loading them onto the truck. I stared at him incredulously.

"Do you mean the outgoing chancellor of the State University of New York and incoming U.S. commissioner of Education for the whole country is driving his own U-Haul to Washington?" I blurted.

"Yes, sir!" he said proudly. "It's a lot cheaper."

Boyer, a modest man, never figured he was too big a guy to move himself.

With the rain falling harder outside the big picture window, we pulled up a couple of boxes near the single lamp that had been left unpacked and sat down for the interview. It was a bizarre scene. As we were winding up, a bolt of lightning crackled outside and lit up the room. Then, a rumble of thunder shook the house. The lamp flickered and went out. Laughing and somewhat embarrassed, Boyer fished a flashlight from somewhere and we finished in the dark. He then used that flashlight to escort me to the door. I wished him luck and that was that. I heard later on that Boyer and his U-Haul made it safely to his new home in Reston, Va., but not before a flat tire somewhere in New Jersey.

Imagine the look of disbelief that might have come over the state trooper's face when he stopped behind the disabled truck and Boyer told him he was the new U.S. commissioner of Education.

"Yeah, right! And I'm Walter Mondale," the trooper might have responded.

Gov. Hugh Carey was one of the nicest guys and smartest politicians I covered. He wasn't flashy. He didn't have grandiose ideas. He never got a chance to build huge edifices like one of his predecessors, Nelson Rockefeller did. Carey inherited the financial mess left over from the binge spending of the Rockefeller years and devoted much energy and a lot of penny pinching over his two terms as governor to getting it straightened out. In 1975, Carey helped save New York City from bankruptcy through the creation of the Municipal Assistance Corporation, the so-called Big MAC, and appointed Wall Street financier Felix Rohatyn to chair it. Big MAC sold bonds to provide the city with badly needed funds and managed its fiscal affairs with a tight fist, eventually bringing it back to solvency. It was the New York City financial crisis, and the federal government's initial refusal to provide bailout funds, that prompted the now-legendary Oct. 30, 1975 New York Daily News headline, "FORD

TO CITY: DROP DEAD!" Ford, of course, was then-President Gerald Ford, whose vice president at the time, ironically, was none other than Rockefeller, under whose watch as governor the state's financial mess took root. While the headline triggered a furor, and a wave of anger toward the Republican president, Washington eventually provided loan guarantees for the city. But it didn't help Ford in the 1976 presidential race. New York gave its 41 electoral votes to Jimmy Carter, a Georgia peanut farmer, who went on to win the election.

Carey, the father of 14 children, was a widower most of the time he was governor. The New York media always played up his dates with various women. On occasion he went out with Ethel Kennedy, widow of the late Robert F. Kennedy. He later married millionaire condominium developer Evangeline Gouletas. But during his early governorship his most steady date was Anne Ford Uzielli, the jet-setting, attractive blonde daughter of auto magnate Henry Ford II. At one point it was reported that Carey, then 59, and Ford Uzielli, 35, were about to be engaged. But she told reporters it wasn't so. The buzz in the Albany press corps newsroom was that Carey leaked the story to help persuade her to say yes. But after that, the relationship cooled.

However, one memorable public evening Carey spent with Ford was at a gala fundraiser in October 1978, when the governor was running for re-election. The black-tie dinner was held in the gold-gilded ballroom of the Waldorf Astoria Hotel on Manhattan's posh East Side and featured as headliner none other than Frank Sinatra. The well-heeled crowd of about 1,500 paid $1,000 a ticket, raising $1.5 million for a campaign that Carey won handily over former Republican Assembly Speaker Perry Duryea, a silver-haired lobster businessman from Montauk on the seaward eastern tip of Long Island. The diners stood and applauded when Carey and Ford, looking very much in love, walked in hand-in-hand and took their seats at the round table front and center on the ballroom floor. There was no head table on the stage, as there are at most political dinners. The stage was taken up by the orchestra, led by Don Costa. Reporters were relegated to stand and watch the show from a balcony far above the floor.

But the view was panoramic and turned out to be spectacular. When the diners settled down and finally took their seats - political crowds like to mingle and schmooze, see and be seen - the ballroom went dark, triggering a surprised murmur from the gathering. Then, small spotlights strategically placed high above the floor lit up and beamed down, illuminating the centerpiece on each table, branches of orange-berried bittersweet in glass, round-bottomed vases with tall, thin necks. The effect was so stunning the crowd broke into spontaneous applause. At the same moment, the orchestra, still in the dark except for those little golden lights on the music stands, began playing a vamp that has now become the familiar lead-in to a song Sinatra made famous, "New York, New York." Then, a huge spotlight sent rays down to the center of the floor where the tuxedoed Sinatra magically appeared and broke into song, "Start spreading the news......"

The audience loved it, and gave Sinatra a standing ovation when he finished, quite rare after the singing of one song, especially a song the audience was not familiar with. As Sinatra said, after the applause died down, the song was introduced a few months earlier in the movie "New York, New York" by Liza Minnelli and he only began singing it a week before, when he played Radio City Music Hall. We all know the rest of the story. In the 27 years since then it has become one of Sinatra's signature songs.

Sinatra went on to sing other songs with New York themes such as "Autumn in New York," "Manhattan" and "New York, New York, a Wonderful Town," a song he sang with Gene Kelly and Jules Munchen in the 1949 classic movie "On the Town."

The fact that Carey was able to get Sinatra to appear at a fund-raiser for him was a tribute in itself. Sinatra had pretty much sworn off the political scene since the early 1960s after his close relationship with President John F. Kennedy went sour. When Kennedy decided to run for president, Sinatra was an early backer. Then-Kennedy brother-in-law Peter Lawford, a member of Sinatra's notorious Rat Pack, recruited the singer to help with Kennedy's 1960 campaign. Sinatra went all out. He headlined fundraisers, hit the campaign trail and even recorded Kennedy jingles that were aired as campaign ads. And when Kennedy won, Sinatra planned and emceed the celebrity-studded gala show staged in Washington the night before the inauguration. But when Kennedy made his brother Robert attorney general, the friendship with Sinatra began to fall apart. Robert told the president he had to cool it because of Sinatra's alleged mob connections. That meant the president had to cancel a long-planned visit to Sinatra's desert home in Palm Springs, Calif., which was scheduled for

March 24-26 1962. To add insult to injury, Kennedy stayed at the nearby home of Bing Crosby and used the excuse that the Secret Service thought security was better there. Sinatra didn't buy it. He had a concrete helicopter pad installed in his yard to accommodate Marine One for the president's arrival. When he got the news that Kennedy wasn't coming after all, he angrily went out back with a sledgehammer and vented his frustrations on the helipad. The snub not only cooled Sinatra's relationship with the president, it also caused him to cut Peter Lawford out of his circle of friends.

Two years after the Carey fundraiser, Sinatra returned to politics to help win the election of a Republican, Ronald Reagan, an old Hollywood friend. To show his appreciation, Reagan in 1982 invited Sinatra and Perry Como to the White House to sing at a State Dinner in honor of the president of Italy, Allesandro Pertini. Sinatra was touched by the invitation. Unlike Kennedy, Reagan was not afraid of the singer's alleged mob connections. A friend was a friend.

Not long after the Sinatra gala, the Carey-Ford Uzielli relationship ended. Later, the gossip columnists began buzzing about a new Carey girlfriend, Evangeline Gouletas, a dark-haired Greek-American millionaire businesswoman with extravagant taste in designer clothes and stylish hats. She also had three or four or five former husbands, depending upon who was counting. But Carey seemed smitten by the sultry Gouletas, or "Engie," as friends called her. They met in Washington at the Reagan inauguration in January 1981. The New York tabloids were awash in photos of the glittering couple as they wined and dined in Manhattan's most chic restaurants - LeCirque, La Cote Basque and Twenty One. Carey behaved like a puppy in love. He beamed from ear to ear, joked with reporters and seemed to be walking on air. He dyed his gray hair, but it turned out an odd shade of orange. You know the look. Carey walked into a Red Room news conference in the State Capitol in Albany sporting his new do and an immediate snicker rippled through the assembled cadre of reporters.

"He looks like a fox," growled the irascible Jerry Alan of the *Buffalo Evening News.* A wave of laughter swept the room.

Carey, who heard the remark and knew what the laughing was about, played right into the reporters' hands. Pulling out the three little steps hidden in one of the drawers of the governor's massive ceremonial mahogany desk, he climbed to its glass top and began to do a little toe dance.

"It's spring! It's spring!" he sang as he pirouetted.

He attributed his miraculous hair-color change to overactive "sebaceous roots" and blithely kept up the joke throughout the questioning. Carey could take a joke as well as dish one out.

The governor's sarcastic humor was in full form one day when a news conference was about to begin and Arthur Greenspan, the rather rotund *New York Post* reporter, was still standing and chatting with his colleagues. Impatient to begin, Carey snapped, "Arthur! Pull up a couple of chairs and sit down."

Carey and Gouletas had a whirlwind courtship. Less than three months after they met, Carey, 62, and Gouletas, 44, were engaged and married, tying the knot on Carey's birthday, April 11, 1981. They were married in New York City, but later in the day flew to Albany where a huge celebration was held on the Empire State Plaza. The bridal couple made a grand entrance, greeted by the cheering throng as they walked up the red-carpeted stairs of the New York State Museum, a layered structure of white marble that looks like a wedding cake whose intricate icing has hardened to stone.

About nine months later, in January 1982, I received a call one afternoon from Carey's press secretary, Jill Schuker, telling me the governor would like to see me at 5 p.m. in his second-floor Capitol office. I was stunned. I never had been summoned to his office before in the six years I had been in Albany. So I naturally figured I must have done something wrong or written something the governor didn't like. I asked Schuker what was up, but all she would say is that the governor just wanted to see me. Nervous and on edge, I walked down the elegant stone staircase from the Capitol Press Room on the third floor to Carey's office one floor below and approached his receptionist. Just then, Schuker stepped out from Carey's inner office and told me to take a seat, the governor would be with me in a minute. She walked back in, leaving me to absently thumb through the New York State *Conservationist* magazines lined up neatly on a coffee table in front of me.

"What does he want?" I kept asking myself.

After about five minutes, Schuker came out and wordlessly waved me in. As I passed by her, I saw Carey, in white shirt and tie, sitting at his desk. He rose to greet me as Schuker left, closing the door behind her. Carey and I were alone. "Here it comes," I thought as we shook hands and sat down, he in a black leather, high-backed chair, me in a wooden armchair on the opposite side of his desk. He came right to the point. "I want to give you a news story before I give it to anyone else," he said.

"What is it?" I asked.

"I am not going to run for re-election this year," Carey answered directly.

I chuckled, figuring it was a joke. "Right," I said almost sarcastically.

"No, really," he responded. "I have decided not to seek a third term, and I am telling you first because I remember a kindness you extended to me when I was criticized in the press for using the state plane to carry my children from Albany to New York and to my home on Shelter Island."

"Kindness?" I asked myself. I had written a column saying that while Carey was being bashed for wasting taxpayer money transporting his two sons, who were still in high school in Albany, to spend weekends with him in New York, it seemed like a legitimate expense since he is governor 24 hours a day, seven days a week, even on weekends. And whether the children were flown downstate to be with him, or he was flown back to Albany to be with them, it was all part of the job. That's it.

Years later, in Washington, I wrote a similar piece defending then-Vice President Dan Quayle, who was criticized for flying Air Force Two to the Masters Golf Tournament in Augusta, Ga. I noted that while several corporate executives offered to fly Quayle down on their own private aircraft, Quayle, as vice president, for security reasons, was not allowed to fly on anything but military aircraft provided by the U.S. government.

Anyway, Carey, thanked me again for the "kindness," and returned the favor by giving me a scoop, which I was later instructed by Schuker to attribute to a high-ranking Carey administration official. Incredulous at my good fortune, I ran upstairs and began writing my story, first breathlessly calling my editors to tell them what I had. They didn't believe me. I couldn't tell them my source, but I assured them that the source was close enough to the governor to know. They still were apprehensive. They didn't see anything about it on the *Associated Press* or *United Press International* wires. How could I have something they don't have? Getting more nervous by the minute, I banged out the story and sent it in. It went out over the Gannett wire by about 7 p.m. to all Gannett-owned newspapers around the country as well as to those in cities in New York State -

Rochester, Niagara Falls, Binghamton, Elmira, Ithaca, Utica, Saratoga Springs, Poughkeepsie, White Plains and Yonkers among them. But even then, editors in those cities reading the story coming off the Gannett wire were slow to believe it. They didn't see it on the *AP* and *UPI* wires either and worried about my story being wrong. As a result, some papers used my exclusive and some did not. The main wire services moved the story at 11 p.m., five hours after my first report. But it made believers of those Gannett editors whose papers had not already gone to press by then. Sadly, however, some Gannett editors used the *AP* or *UPI* pieces, ignoring mine, while others used mine. It took the edge off of my scoop, which I was feeling pretty good about. In the end, I was disappointed. But that's the news business: Some days you win, and some days you lose.

72

A Newspaper is Born

Late in 1981, Alan H. Neuharth, the flamboyant, entrepreneurial chairman and CEO of Gannett Co. Inc., the media conglomerate I was working for, announced to a roomful of company mangers that the corporation, after making an extensive marketing study, would create a national newspaper - USA TODAY. The Gannett managers gave their dapper chief a standing ovation. But outside that Washington, D.C. hotel ballroom where the meeting was held, the news was largely greeted with a laugh not only among investment and financial analysts, but also the media community itself. "It will never fly," was the collective doomsday prediction.

The doubters had good reason. The United States never had a truly national newspaper. Newspapers such as the *Wall Street Journal* and the *New York Times* could be found in major cities around the country, but neither was ever considered a truly national daily newspaper. Most newspapers were generally focused on a particular city or region, serving the parochial interests of those who lived and worked in that area. Dow Jones & Co., publisher of the *Wall Street Journal*, made an attempt to create a general-audience national newspaper in 1962 when it launched the *National Observer*. The *Observer* was an attractive, well-designed and attractive weekly publication that featured some of the finest reporting and writing in the news business. But it never really caught on much beyond a loyal cadre of elite readers that included business leaders, college professors, East Coast intellectuals and journalism students. Weekly circulation peaked at 560,000 in 1973, but had dropped to 400,000 when Dow Jones shut it down in 1977, 15 years after its much-heralded launch.

But less than five years after the *National Observer's* demise, Neuharth boldly announced Gannett was going to create a daily national newspaper that would be sold all across the country. John Morton, a former reporter at the *National Observer*, and now a leading media analyst, wrote in *American Journalism Review* in 1982, shortly before USA TODAY's debut, "The list of large-circulation daily newspapers successfully established since World War II is not just short, it is nonexistent....A national daily newspaper seems like a way to lose a lot of money in a hurry."

Peter Prichard wrote in his book, "The Making of McPaper," a history of USA TODAY'S startup, that the investor community greeted the news by selling off Gannett stock. On Dec. 14, 1981, the day before Neuharth's announcement, Gannett shares were trading at 38 1/2. On March 15, three months later, they hit 29 1/2, a 23 percent drop. That translated into a $477 million loss in market value.

But for reporters like me, working for Gannett newspapers or news bureaus mostly in small and medium-size cities, a new national newspaper sounded exciting, an opportunity to cover bigger stories and be read nationwide. So when Neuharth began assembling a staff to get the newspaper off the ground, he called for volunteers from Gannett newspapers and the *Gannett News Service* to come to Washington, D.C. to join the team. Volunteering did not mean you were automatically selected. Neuharth and a task force of top company officials, including my *Gannett News Service* boss, John Curley, screened the list and made their picks. I was one of 141 who made the cut. Here was the deal the company offered to those Gannett employees willing to join what came to be known as The Launch Team:

Move to the Washington, D.C. area on a trial basis for a minimum of six months. Stay in rent-free studio apartments conveniently situated next door to the USA TODAY building. Receive $120 a week expense money and one free, round-trip airline ticket home every month.

Moreover, the trial run was risk-free. Your pay at your permanent job would continue and your position would be held for you in case you decided you didn't want to stay after the six months were up. You also could be sent back to your old job if USA TODAY editors decided they didn't want you to stay. It happened to a number of reporters, most of whom previously had only experienced success in their careers. They were crushed by the rejection. And, of course, your old job would be waiting for you in case USA TODAY flopped before the six months were up.

But the adventure was not without personal hardship. I was married with four daughters, one 15 years old and triplets who were three. That meant that my wife, Carol, would be stuck caring for the children, a difficult chore without me around to help. But she knew that I considered the USA TODAY venture a good career move and was entirely encouraging and supportive. Had she not been, I would have never done it.

We agreed that I would come home to Albany most weekends, using the weekly expense money to pay for the air fare. In those days you could fly round-trip from Washington to Albany, N.Y. for about $125. So every Friday afternoon, after I finished work, I would take a cab to Washington National Airport, now Reagan National, and fly home. My wife and kids would meet me at the Albany Airport. Back then, nearly 20 years before September 11, families and friends could greet incoming passengers at the arrival gate. Each week, when I stepped off the jetway, there were my triplets, Aimee, Rebecca and Carlin, screeching with delight to see their returning dad. It was quite a spectacle to see those three little girls, all dressed alike, trying to hug my knees at once. Some passengers would actually stop to applaud a scene that to them seemed heartwarming. Being only three years old, the triplets weren't quite sure where I went all week and where I was coming from. Somehow, they concluded among themselves that I lived at the airport.

Life on the Launch Team was not what I expected. The days were long. The pressure was heavy, stories we wrote were never good enough for the editors and the uncertainty about where our brave new project was headed weighed heavily on everyone from the top bosses giving the unborn newspaper a direction to the young news assistants who mostly ran errands. One news assistant who years later was promoted to reporter often joked about how he once was sent out by one of the woman editors to buy her a pair of pantyhose. He used to blush when he told the story.

The new USA TODAY headquarters was in a sleek, silver-gray, oval-shaped 33-story building in Arlington, Va. just across the Potomac River from the Kennedy Center. The now-familiar blue "USA TODAY" logo crowned the top rim of the building and seemed close enough to touch by passengers of incoming planes making their landing approach to National Airport. From our 14th floor offices we had a panoramic view of Washington, D.C., with the familiar white dome of the Capitol on the far horizon, the majestic 555-foot Washington Monument jutting skyward from the middle of the landscape and the white marble of the Lincoln Memorial just below and to the right. We also could see three bridges crossing the Potomac carrying cars into D.C. - the arches of the Key Bridge linking Virginia to Georgetown on our left, the less-scenic Roosevelt Bridge just below us and the Memorial Bridge to our right, a span made famous in those November 1963 pictures showing John F. Kennedy's funeral procession crossing over from Washington to Arlington National Cemetery. "Spectacular" is the way visitors would describe it when they caught their first glimpse of the view we came to take for granted.

In August 1982, I went to work as a reporter for USA TODAY, a newspaper still nearly two months away from its debut. After getting oriented, the newcomers were introduced to our newsroom. We were surprised to find it in the late stages of completion, with ceiling lights and wires exposed and workmen on ladders arrayed all around us. Our desks were sectioned off on long white benches, with bookshelves spanning the length of the bench in the place that would be the splashboard if it was a sink. Long tubes of overhead lighting extended the length of the benches above the bookshelves, causing someone to dub the setup a "salad bar." Rather than built-in storage drawers below the desktops, each reporter was assigned a maroon metal cabinet on wheels with three drawers which could be slid under the desk. Watching people roll these squatty little portable carts around the newsroom as new desks were assigned reminded someone of R2-D2, the little robot in "Star Wars." It should have been a clue that before the dust was settled there would be a lot of games of musical chairs. And there were. To this day, the cabinets, now replaced by less-gaudy blue and black ones, are referred to as "R2-D2s."

Of the 218 professional journalists on staff when USA TODAY began publication on Sept. 15, 1982, 141 were loaners from other Gannett papers and the *Gannett News Service*, where I worked. Another 77 staff professionals were hired from other non-Gannett publications, including newspapers in Charlotte, N.C., New York, Baltimore, Detroit and Miami. Overall, the original staffers came from 29 states, with the New York contingent the largest, comprising 37.

Peter Prichard, an original staffer, wrote in "The Making of McPaper," that Neuharth figured creating a news staff with diverse geographic backgrounds would be good for the nascent newspaper. Prichard quoted Neuharth as saying several years later, "Our people from across the USA came with a fresh approach to journalistic assumptions, different from those that had developed through the years primarily in Washington and New York. What they brought - and what produced the initial (critical) reaction from editors and publishers - was change."

"Change" was putting it mildly. The first edition of USA TODAY that appeared in those now familiar television-like-white-and-blue boxes took readers and the newspaper world by surprise. It featured full-color pictures and charts on the front page, then almost unheard of in the news business, but now a staple, even at the tradition-bound *New York Times*, long known as the "Gray Lady" of the industry. The lead story, just seven paragraphs long, ran under the headline, "America's Princess Grace dies in Monaco." It recounted movie star Grace Kelly's death in an auto crash the day before. To its left was a dramatic color photo of a burning Spantax charter airliner, carrying many Americans, that crashed in Spain. A series of fiery photos was taken by a passenger who escaped. USA TODAY paid $5,000 to print two of them. And in keeping with Neuharth's much-criticized news philosophy of not always emphasizing the negative, pejoratively dubbed "The Journalism of Hope," the headline, written by Neuharth on his old manual typewriter read, "Miracle: 327 survive, 55 die."

Also on the front page was a five-paragraph story written by pollster Louis Harris, whose firm was then owned by Gannett. Harris, once John F. Kennedy's pollster, reported on the primary results from the day before and glanced ahead to the November congressional elections. Another story, nine paragraphs long, was headlined, "Your kid REALLY may be sick of school." It focused on a psychiatric study of children's reactions to school.

The cover story, which was meant to be the signature piece of the front page - longer, more in depth and dealing with a major issue of the day - was written by me. It illuminated an issue then just beginning to emerge, but still much discussed nearly a quarter-century later - suburban sprawl and the problems it brings. Since then, a cover story has appeared on every front page of USA TODAY. But I will always have the honor of writing the first one. Coincidentally, I wrote the cover story that appeared on Page One on the 15th anniversary issue, Sept. 15, 1997, causing one new editor to ask, "Do you write all the anniversary cover stories?" The answer was no.

On the night that the first edition of USA TODAY went to press, Neuharth, in keeping with his flamboyant style, chartered buses to take the staffers out to the printing plant in suburban Springfield, Va.. and greet the first copies as they rolled off the presses. On the buses, tuxedoed waiters served champagne and canapés. On the way back, our fresh copies of the paper in hand, Neuharth, sitting across the aisle from me, slapped the front page and said, "Benedetto, writing the first cover story is going to make you famous." I chuckled and replied, "I wish."

Fifteen years later, while being interviewed for an anniversary video on the early years of the paper, I recounted Neuharth's prediction of fame for me, and added, "I am still waiting." When aired at an anniversary dinner hosted by Neuharth, by then retired from Gannett, the sarcastic remark drew a big laugh from the audience, including Neuharth. Incidentally, as of this writing, I am the only reporter on the original news staff who is still a reporter on the staff some 23 years later. Others on that original staff were cut, returned to their old jobs, left for other papers, stuck around a while and went to work in other departments or became editors. When I tell people that I am the lone original, I add, "You would think I could get a promotion." But the truth is, I always wanted to be a reporter, nothing else. And I haven't changed my mind.

That first edition of USA TODAY was greeted with almost unanimous derision, not only by news media critics and academics, but also newspaper editors, including some of the most prominent ones. "Too gaudy," "not serious" and "too frivolous" were among the first criticisms of the upstart new kid on the block. But readers loved it and bought it.

Many editors questioned the decision to lead the paper with the death of Princess Grace and not the assassination of Lebanese President-elect Bashir Gemayel, which also took place that day. Most other major papers led with Gemayel's death, USA TODAY put it inside the paper. The decision to go with Princess Grace was made by Neuharth after he stopped in a bar and heard people there talking about her death and not about Gemayel. Prichard, in his book on the USA TODAY startup, said Neuharth later explained his choice this way: "Gemayel was Lebanon's president, but Princess Grace was our princess; she belonged to the people of the USA."

Neuharth also used to often say that USA TODAY was designed for readers across the USA, and not for elitist newspaper editors in Washington and New York. But the critics were relentless. As Prichard noted in his book, within a week of the first issue, Ray White, a former editor of

Washington Journalism Review, wrote in *Adweek*, "It is difficult to define news in such a way that Princess Grace's death is more important than Gemayel's."

Maybe so. But the Neuharth formula, despite its detractors, turned out to be a winner. USA TODAY has grown from a glimmer in Neuharth's eye to the Number One daily newspaper in the nation, selling an average 2.3 million papers a day, more than twice the number sold by either the *New York Times* or the *Washington Post*, many of whose reporters and editors are among the last bastions of USA TODAY non-believers. Journalism professors, especially those in the elite colleges, have also been slow to come around. Many often go out of their way to tell me they rarely read USA TODAY, but always read the *New York Times*. Or they criticize USA TODAY for not being more like the *New York Times*, to which I reply, "If there was a market out there for another *New York Times*, the *New York Times* would be selling 2.3 million papers a day across the country, and not USA TODAY."

Those early days as a reporter for a fledgling newspaper were sometimes daunting as I tried to make contact with political figures or government officials for stories I was working on. A phone call to the office of a congressman or a mayor would almost always produce the same suspicious question when I identified myself as a reporter from USA TODAY.

"USA what?" or "U.S. Aid?" the receptionist would ask with puzzlement.

Often, when leaving a message for a press secretary of the official I was seeking, it would not be answered unless I persisted and made several calls urging a response. Even then, the response would seldom be from the official I was seeking, but an underling dispatched to find out what the pest wanted.

In August 1982, when we were still not publishing, but producing prototype or dummy issues as practice runs, I made a call to an official in Colorado state government for a story I was working on. Even though the public would never see these stories we were producing for the prototypes, we still reported them as if they would be read across the country the next day. By pure luck, I got the official I was seeking on the phone, and he graciously gave me the economic statistics I needed for my "story." But even in the prototype days, our editors were picky in the extreme, often asking reporters to produce obscure statistics that were hard to uncover - an oddity that would carry over once the newspaper began actual publication. I had to make several callbacks to the Colorado official to get additional information demanded by my editor. On the third call, the official said to me, "Wait a minute. You are working on a story for a prototype, right?"

"Right," I replied.

"And this story is going to go into a newspaper that the public will never see, right?"

"Right," I repeated.

"Well, then," he concluded, "Why bother me. Why don't you just fake it?"

Thankfully, it never occurred to me to fake anything - prototype or not. News reporting is too high a public trust to resort to such tactics. Journalists who break that trust deserve whatever punishment they get.

But one illustrative incident of USA TODAY's early fascination with obscure information occurred in early December 1982, when the paper was not yet three months old. That morning, when official Washington was just getting to work, a man wearing a nylon jumpsuit and a motorcycle helmet drove a truck up to the base of the 555-foot Washington Monument, said his vehicle was loaded with explosives and threatened to blow it up. He was Norman Mayer, a lonely drifter who was identified by police as an anti-nuclear-arms activist. A sign on the side of his truck read, "#1 PRIORITY: BAN NUCLEAR WEAPONS."

I was dispatched to the scene to cover the dramatic event and spent most of the day there while the man and the police continued their standoff. As 5 p.m. approached and it was getting dark, another USA TODAY reporter and friend, Sam Meddis, relieved me so I could get back to the office and write the story. When I returned to the newsroom, I was told to take a seat at the editors' desk and start writing. I was positioned there because all of the editors, from Neuharth on down, wanted to be involved, and thus began hovering over my shoulders as I began to write.

But as I starting clicking the buttons on the keyboard, I noticed that there was a lot of frantic fretting swirling around me over reporters who were trying to uncover data that their editors had insisted they produce. One reporter was ordered to find out exactly how many federal employees had been evacuated from office buildings around the threatened Monument and sent home. The *Associated Press* was reporting one number. *United Press International* was reporting another. Our editors wanted to know precisely how many people were evacuated. And when the reporter assigned to unearth the truth came back and said he was having no luck, the editors grew more frantic and more insistent. Finally, Bob Dubill, a veteran newsman and a top editor with the *Gannett News Service* who had been dispatched to USA TODAY to impose some calm on what was becoming a frazzled newsroom, heard enough. He pulled himself up out of his chair to his full 6-3 height, pounded his fist on the top of his computer monitor for extra emphasis and bellowed in a booming voice that was his signature: "SEVERAL THOUSAND FEDERAL EMPLOYEES WERE EVACUATED AND SENT HOME! AND I DON'T WANT TO HEAR ANOTHER WORD ABOUT IT!"

The bustling room went silent, shocked by the outburst. But reason prevailed and we got back to reporting the story of the man threatening to blow up the Monument. Shortly afterward, all eyes in the newsroom darted to the ceiling-mounted TVs. CNN was televising the monument ordeal live. Under the cover of darkness, the man got into his truck, turned on the headlights and began driving down the hill and toward Constitution Avenue, about 150 yards to the north. Police later said they viewed the truck as a "moving time bomb" headed for downtown Washington. Unbeknownst to reporters on the scene, federal police sharpshooters, under the darkness of night, had moved into the shadows of the Mall. When the truck began moving, portable floodlights lit up the scene and police opened fire. Mayer was hit four times, twice in the head, and killed. His truck turned out to have no explosives in it. A sad ending to a very unusual day.

Dubill, the editor who created calm out of chaos so the story could be written, would later go on to become the executive editor of USA TODAY and one of its steadiest and most respected leaders. His ready smile, deep laugh, insistence on fairness and dogged pursuit of the truth, wherever it led, were his hallmarks in a time where fairness is sometimes seen as a quaint notion and truth can often float, like the dollar.

Sam Meddis, the reporter who relieved me at the Monument, became a close friend. He now is a top editor at USA TODAY.com, the newspaper's popular website. He and I still laugh about our first Thanksgiving at USA TODAY. Everyone had to work on a slow news day. To keep me busy, they had me chase down a story about Louisiana oysters, a key ingredient

82

in some turkey stuffing recipes, which had gone bad. Meddis and I went to lunch at Roy Rogers, the fast-food hamburger restaurant which was then across the street from our offices. Our footsteps echoed on the tile floors. We were the only customers there. And the hamburgers were cold. Feeling pretty lonely, I put my burger to my lips and took a bite. Meddis looked across the table at me and quipped, "Well, Mr. Bigshot, how do you like your new job?"

On the front page of USA TODAY on Sept. 15, 1982, Alan Neuharth, its visionary founder, explained the new national newspaper's philosophy and guiding principles:

"USA TODAY begins its reach across the USA with a commitment to serve as a clear and true mirror that reflects all of our nation's images, inspects all of our problems, projects all of our opportunities and respects all of our people.

"USA TODAY hopes to serve as a forum for better understanding and unity to make the USA truly one nation."

I believed in those statements then, and I believe in them now. I have tried my best to live up to them in a turbulent news media environment of ferment and change. And for the most part, the newspaper has, too.

USA TODAY's critics persist. But I can say something that most journalists can not say: I helped start a newspaper, a good one, at that.

REFERENCES
Prichard, Peter. 1987. "The Making of McPaper," Kansas City-New York, Andrews, McMeel and Parker.

"Politicians are People, Too"

Trivial statistics aside, it was difficult in those early USA TODAY days to get political figures to respond positively to my inquires. Many saw no advantage in being quoted in a newspaper they thought no one would be reading, let alone heard of. So I developed a soft spot in my heart for those who did respond and cooperate. There were many who opened their doors to me in those early years, several of whom went on to bigger and better things. Among them: Mayors Henry Cisneros of San Antonio, Harold Washington of Chicago, George Voinovich of Cleveland, W. Wilson Goode of Philadelphia, Ray Flynn of Boston, Terry Goddard of Phoenix, Helen Boosalis of Lincoln, Neb., Ernest "Dutch" Morial and son Marc Morial, of New Orleans and Charles Royer of Seattle, a former TV reporter who could sympathize with a journalist's need for access. I remember them all as hard-working public servants who always had their cities and its residents at heart.

Welcoming governors who became national figures: Arizona's Bruce Babbitt, Tennessee's Lamar Alexander, Massachusetts' Michael Dukakis, Florida's Bob Graham, Virginia's Charles Robb, Pennsylvania's Dick Thornburgh, Vermont's Madeleine Kunin, Colorado's Roy Romer, Nebraska's Kay Orr, Arkansas' Bill Clinton and Texas' George W. Bush.

Like all good officeholders, these mayors and governors kept things moving forward, not back. Maybe not in giant steps all the time, but through prudent compromise and artful persuasion always forward, despite some tough odds that included limited funds, racial unrest, intractable poverty and a political opposition that never let up.

Harold Washington, who made history in 1983 by being elected Chicago's first black mayor with 51 percent of the vote, suffered an untimely death from a heart attack in 1987, shortly after winning a second term. With his wavy white hair and dapper moustache, Washington proved to be a very friendly fellow who was welcoming to me when I went to the Windy City to cover his re-election campaign in 1987. He even let me ride in his limousine for an interview between campaign stops one Sunday, much to the upset of local reporters who had been desperately trying, with no luck, to get an interview for weeks. Washington and I bonded a year earlier when he was in Washington, D.C. on business and I went to his hotel suite on a sunny Saturday afternoon in May to interview him. He was watching a Chicago White Sox-New York Yankees baseball game on TV. Washington being a White Sox fan, had trouble tearing himself away from the game. And I, being a Yankees fan, had trouble focusing on the interview myself. When the interview was over, he invited me to stay for the rest of the game, and I did. It was a great time with a great guy. We discussed everything from the finer points of baseball to our family roots. He came from a long line of Baptist ministers, breaking the string to become a lawyer, and later a congressman, before winning the Chicago mayoralty. He showed great interest in my Italian-American background.

So Washington knew me when I went to Chicago to cover his re-election campaign the following year. During the course of the day he made several political stops, one being a black church that was crowded with supporters, so crowded that there were no seats for the handful of reporters who followed him there. As Washington, whose father and grandfather were preachers, began his passionate speech from the pulpit, I stood against the wall on the left side of the church to listen and take notes. Seated directly across from me was an elderly black woman wearing a hat with a flower on it and a little boy about six or seven looking very neat in a white shirt and clip-on bow tie. I took her to be his grandmother. The woman saw me standing there and turned to the little boy.

"Give the gentleman your seat," she said firmly.

The little boy obediently stood up so I could sit. I was embarassed.

"Oh no, I'm fine here. I can stand. Thank you anyway," I said.

But the grandmother would hear none of it.

"Oh, no," she said. "He has to learn to respect his elders."

So I sat down while the little boy stood. It was humiliating, but still nice to see a grandmother teaching her grandson an important personal lesson he probably never forgot.

I remember going to a black church in San Antonio with Mayor Henry Cisneros, a Mexican-American, in 1986 for a gospel choir festival. Cisneros, his wife Mary Alice and I were the only white people there, but we were warmly received. Cisneros had come to play the piano in accompaniment to one gospel group. He played a spirited piano, but a bit stiffly. He never did get down that back-and-forth rocking motion that I saw other piano players display, sort of Ray Charles style.

I had gone to San Antonio to prepare a profile on Cisneros, who was about to take over as president of the National League of Cities. Two years earlier, he was one of five finalists that Democrat Walter Mondale considered for his running mate in the 1984 presidential election. Cisneros lost out to Geraldine Ferraro, but his being considered thrust him into the national spotlight. Many saw him as a future Texas governor and even president.

While in San Antonio, Cisneros and I got along so well that he invited me for dinner on Tuesday night at the home of his wife's parents, Mexican immigrants who ran a grocery store and bakery. I demurred when he asked me to join the family at dinner, not wanting to intrude. But he insisted. He was driving the car. When we arrived at their home, it was if I had stepped back 30 years to dinner at my grandfather's house. The whole family was there, brothers and sisters of Mary Alice Cisneros and their families. The children were seated in the kitchen, where the women were preparing the meal. The men were seated in the dining room, waiting for the dinner to be served. At the head of the table was Mary Alice's father, quietly holding court and looking proud. I was seated to his left, just as I used to be seated with my grandfather. And I felt as if I was among family, although I only met all of them minutes before. Why did he invite me to dinner with his family? Surely, it crossed my mind that he was trying to influence me to write a favorable piece. Maybe that's what he was hoping. The profile I wrote turned out to be mostly positive. But it was based on the facts, and not on my turning a blind eye toward his negative points.

Years later, Cisneros got involved in a messy extramarital affair with Linda Medlar, who had been a campaign worker and fundraiser for him. His public admission of the affair, and his subsequent leaving of his wife to be with Medlar, only to reconcile later, virtually ended a promising elective political career. Imagine if Cisneros had gone on to become governor of Texas in place of George W. Bush. We could be looking at a Cisneros presidency now, or maybe in 2008, given the growing political power of the Hispanic vote, not to mention his considerable charisma and sharp political skills as a moderate Democrat. But like all of us, politicians sometimes make big mistakes, and those mistakes can be costly to their careers. Cisneros knows that only too well. But that is not the end of the Cisneros story. In 1995, when he wanted to tell his side of the Medlar story to the national media in the latest twist in what had become a highly publicized scandal, he called me and offered the exclusive to USA TODAY. Other national publications and TV networks were clamoring for interviews. But he said he selected me because he trusted me to treat him fairly. And he made it clear to our editors that he would only do the interview if I conducted it.

The Cisneros affair was in the news again because then-Attorney General Janet Reno named a special prosecutor to look into whether he lied under oath in 1993 about cash payments he made to Medlar, who by then was his former lover. The alleged lie came during Senate confirmation hearings on his appointment to be secretary of Housing and Urban Development in the Clinton administration. Everyone expected Cisneros to resign his HUD post when Reno's decision to investigate possible criminal charges against him was announced. But Cisneros decided to stay, and he used his interview with me to tell the nation why. USA TODAY made the interview its March 16, 1995 cover story with a Page One headline that read, "I feel some shame" and below it in a subhead, "Emotional Cisneros describes decision 'to clear my name.'" The story began like this:

> "Henry Cisneros wasn't planning to be on the job today.
>
> "The secretary of Housing and Urban Development says he went to work Tuesday expecting to quit the Cabinet post he held for the past 26 months.
>
> "Attorney General Janet Reno had concluded that Cisneros, once a rising star in the Democratic Party, had lied to the FBI about support payments he had made to a former lover and recommended that a special prosecutor look into potential criminal charges.
>
> " 'I thought I was going to resign,' Cisneros told USA TODAY in an emotional 70-minute interview. 'Believe me, there was a great temptation to take the easy route, which is to step down.'
>
> "Cisneros, cheeks flushing, repeatedly said, 'I made a mistake, a big mistake,' over his affair with one-time aide Linda Medlar, and of his payments to her over 3 1/2 years. Medlar says they totaled $213,000. Cisneros won't give a figure.

"But he described how meetings with White House fellows, his HUD staff, his wife, and finally, a call from President Clinton, convinced him to stay."

My getting that interview illustrates an important point about politicians, a point that I try to impress upon journalism students looking forward to careers in political reporting: Politicians don't expect you to only write favorable stories about them. They would like it, but they don't expect it. They have been around the block a few times and they know that taking their lumps in the media is part of the game, a big part of the game. What makes politicians angry, and causes them to slam the door in your face when you come to call, is a feeling that you have not treated them or reported about them fairly. Shortly after former president George H.W. Bush left the White House, he did an interview with a *Washington Times* reporter about his relationship with the White House Press Corps, a relationship that he felt was more negative than positive. In that interview, the elder Bush singled me out as one of its members who he considered "tough, but fair." A political reporter can not ask for a better testimonial from a politician he has covered.

When I talk to student journalists, I tell them that their reputation is everything. Don't pull punches, but treat politicians fairly. Get their side of the story. Put the story into context. And when you are reporting the words of critics that are unusually harsh, always make sure those criticisms are on the record with their names attached to them. It is not the journalist's job to allow anonymous sources to take shots without standing behind them. My rule: All criticism is made on the record or forget my printing it. My name never was attached to a story that said something like, "One Republican critic of Democratic Sen. John Doe said, 'Sen. Doe is constantly selling out to the political interests and is probably finding a way to hide the money he is taking from them.'" But how many times have you seen anonymous quotes of that nature?

Thankfully, the media are getting tougher these days about the use of anonymous sources. Anonymous sources are valuable to journalists, especially when they are able to bring to light important inside information about government wrongdoing or blatant falsification of the facts. But there is no doubt that over the past three decades, spurred in large part by Watergate, the ultimate anonymous-source story which brought down a president, many journalists have abused the use of anonymous sources in their hope of duplicating the feat. And in the process, they have helped undermine public credibility in the fairness of reporting. It is true that one of the key functions of political journalism is to act as a watchdog on government and bring to light those things public officials might be hiding and the public needs to know. But at the same time, reporters should never lose sight of the fact that the reason why we perform the watchdog function is not to tear governments down and undermine public confidence in them, it is to point out wrongdoing so that that it can be corrected and governments can work better. The goal is better government, not another notch in the gunslinging reporter's belt.

If any mayor deserves to retire the title of "Mr. Nice Guy," it is Joe Riley Jr., the polite and dapper - he wears gray seersucker suits, striped ties and white-buck shoes in summer - Democratic mayor of Charleston, S.C. Riley has been in office since 1975, more than three decades at this writing. You can't survive that long in no-holds-barred city politics without people liking you. They like him so much in Charleston that they named the city's minor league baseball stadium, home of the Charleston River Dogs, after him. Known officially as Joseph P. Riley Jr. Park, it is affectionately referred to by River Dogs fans as "The Joe."

I liked Riley immediately when I met him back in the early 1980s through his work with the U.S. Conference of Mayors, an organization of chief city executives that he served as president of in 1986-87. He was generous with his time with me, despite my representing USA TODAY, a paper that he was largely unfamiliar with when I first happened to contact him.

My fondest memory of Riley came when he was installed as president of the mayors' conference at the group's 1986 annual meeting, which was held in San Juan, Puerto Rico. With the ballroom of the San Juan Hilton jammed with more than 500 applauding mayors, Riley approached the podium and began to deliver his inaugural speech in Spanish. *"Buenos dias, damas y cabelleros.....,"* he began in a kind of high pitched, nervous voice that sounded even higher when his Southern drawl was combined with Spanish. With the introduction and nod to the host city over, he proceeded in English for a couple of minutes, and then suddenly stopped. Looking puzzled, he said, "Oh, sorry." He then shyly explained that he had forgotten to turn his tape recorder on to preserve his words for his father. Then, he turned on the recorder and resumed his speech: *"Buenos dias, damas y cabelleros.....,"* he repeated, starting from the top. His fellow mayors roared with laughter, and then applauded with affection.

Another politician high on my good-guy list is George Voinovich, the former Republican mayor of Cleveland, who later went on to become Ohio governor and then U.S. senator. As mayor, in early 1983, he warmly welcomed me to his city even though USA TODAY had not begun publication there yet. I had been sent to Cleveland as part of an advance group of three USA TODAY reporters, exaggeratingly dubbed a "blitz team," to put together some Cleveland-related stories that could run in the paper when it began publication there some three or four weeks down the road. I figured my best bet for story tips was to start reading the Cleveland newspapers to get up to speed on what was going on there, and being a political reporter, make contact with the mayor, who was Voinovich. I called his office ice cold. He never heard of me and was only vaguely familiar with USA TODAY, which by then was only nine months old. But after making a request for an interview to his press secretary, Claire Rosocco, Voinovich quickly said yes.

So on my first day in Cleveland, I went straight to the mayor's office for a chat with the top man himself. Voinovich was hardly the vision of a big-city mayor that Hollywood might have conjured up. He was short and soft-spoken, polite and nicely dressed in a brown suit and tie. His large, but somewhat dark City Hall office had an old oriental rug on the floor. A somewhat formal fellow, he kept his jacket on when we talked. I also noticed that he had a sad look in his eyes, which focused sharply on his visitor during the conversation.

I later learned that Voinovich had a reason for the sad eyes, which he still displays today, some 22 years later, as he continues his long career of public service. In 1979, just four years before I met him, his daughter, Molly Agnes, 9, the youngest of his four children, was killed when she was hit by a car while walking back from lunch to Oliver Hazard Perry School. Every year since, George and Janet Voinovich have donated money to the Cleveland public schools in honor of their daughter and return to Perry School for annual observances, which usually feature singing by the school's choir and special programs put on by the students.

Voinovich was more than helpful in our first meeting. He gave me a list of people I should talk to and said he would be glad to put together a lunch to introduce me to some "community leaders." That lunch, held in the City Club of Cleveland, on the top floor of one of the city's tallest skyscrapers, high above Euclid Avenue, featured not just "community leaders," but the top community leaders, including the CEOs of many of Cleveland's big industries and banks. They were there, at Voinovich's invitation, to meet a reporter from a new newspaper coming to town. They were most gracious and willing to assist in any way they could. I am sure that introduction helped build some good will and get USA TODAY off on the right foot in Cleveland. It was a case of a mayor going far beyond the call of duty to extend a helping hand. It happens a lot in cities all over the country. In today's highly charged political atmosphere, there is little room in the news media for such stories.

I continued to stay in contact with Voinovich as I covered mayors and governors in the 1980s. In 1990, I traveled with then-President George H.W. Bush to Cleveland for a fund-raising lunch in support of Voinovich in a downtown. Voinovich was then running for Ohio governor. When the lunch ended, I ran to the men's room. When I came out, I realized the presidential entourage was already leaving. By the time I got outside, the motorcade was pulling away and heading for the airport. I turned to Voinovich, who had accompanied the president outside and told him of my predicament. Although he was no longer mayor, he summoned a police car from across the street and ordered the driver to take me to the airport. I jumped in. The patrolman turned on his lights and siren, radioed ahead to police in the presidential motorcade and said we would be joining them shortly. Within minutes, we were in sight of the motorcade and just tagged on at the end. I made my plane, thanks to Voinovich.

One more quick Voinovich story: It took place in 1996. He was Ohio governor then and Bob Dole was running for the Republican nomination for president. Dole took his campaign to Cleveland, and Voinovich, whose mother was a Slovenian immigrant, took him to a rally at the Slovenian Club on the city's blue-collar east side. The hall was packed with people of Slovenian descent, many of them immigrants. Some women were dressed in native peasant costumes and danced on stage to the music provided by an energetic polka band. The place was rocking and Dole was welcomed heartily with cheers and clapping. Dole, who is known for his low-key persona and dry wit, beamed from ear to ear. He was so taken by the reception that he grabbed one of the women in native costume and danced a jaunty and spirited polka. I had never seen Dole dance before, and never since. Voinovich was a gracious host. He was later disappointed by Dole when the GOP nominee picked Jack Kemp, instead of him, to be his running mate. Voinovich was considered a top contender for the No. 2 spot on the Republican ticket. But it never tempered his enthusiasm in support of Dole's losing candidacy to Bill Clinton. To George Voinovich, loyalty is a virtue.

One of the classiest politicians I met is George McGovern, the former South Dakota Democratic senator who ran for president in 1972, only to be soundly trounced by Richard Nixon. He has a gentle way about him and a voice that is soothing, even when he is being critical. He is a throwback in today's high-voltage political world where voices always seem to be raised and grudges never seem to go away. McGovern never held a grudge against Nixon for the drubbing he took at his hands - 49 states to one. Massachusetts was the only state McGovern carried. He even lost his home state of South Dakota. But despite the humiliation he suffered at Nixon's hands in '72, and his rival's subsequent demise in the Watergate scandal less than two years later, McGovern never publicly gloated over what many saw as his vindication. Instead, McGovern was one of only two Democrats to attend former first lady Pat Nixon's funeral when she died in 1993. The other was Washington lawyer Vernon Jordan, President Clinton's official representative at the funeral.

The Clintons, who were in the White House at that time, did not attend. Very few news outlets made note of McGovern's attendance at the funeral in Yorba Linda, Calif., but the *New York Post* did. I saw the item and decided a few days later to call McGovern and ask him why he bothered to make the cross-country trip from Washington to California to pay his last respects to the wife of his one-time bitter rival. Clearly, the soft-spoken former senator from South Dakota was not one to hold grudges. And it was in a spirit of good will and reconciliation that he said he made the journey.

"I can't tell you I knew Mrs. Nixon well, although I had met her and talked to her briefly on several occasions. But I admired her," he told me. "She was a very unpretentious public figure. She kept her own counsel, and she didn't seem to be engaged in a lot of fanfare or phony public gestures. She maintained her own sense of personal integrity. I wanted to be part of a public ceremony honoring her."

But as he continued, it was clear there was more to his attendance than just honoring a former first lady who he admired. "I think this country needs some reconciliation efforts," he said. "There's just too much intense partisanship, sniping and back-biting. As somebody who has locked horns with Richard Nixon over the years, I thought showing up at that would show some level of reconciliation."

It did, and then some. The Nixon family was overwhelmed in appreciation for the thoughtful gesture of an old political opponent. The gratitude expressed to McGovern by Nixon's daughters, Tricia Cox and Julie Eisenhower, touched him deeply.

"That alone made the trip worthwhile," he said.

After the services, a grief-stricken Nixon spoke privately with the guests.

"George, nice of you to come," he said, according to the *New York Post*.

"Well, she was a great lady," McGovern replied.

"She was a South Dakota girl," Nixon said.

McGovern said he was puzzled by that one, conceding later he was not aware of Mrs. Nixon's South Dakota connection. A check of her biography found that her father met her mother in South Dakota, and they were married there before moving to Nevada, where Mrs. Nixon was born in 1912.

The absence at the funeral of any official members of the Clinton administration, not the usual protocol when a former first lady dies, was viewed by some Republicans as a way of snubbing, or at least trying not to be tainted by associating with Nixon, who was disgraced. Clinton did send the former Air Force One jetliner on which Nixon had flown as president to carry Mrs. Nixon's body home from New Jersey, where they lived, to California, where she was buried. But as I wrote back then in a column for the *Gannett News Service,* "It took a really big man like George McGovern to show that even in the battle-scarred world of big-time partisan politics, there's still room for decency, kindness and a thoughtful gesture - even toward one-time enemies." After that column appeared, McGovern called to thank me for the kind words. It was a gesture in true keeping with his character.

Similar gestures of good will were made in 1995 by New York Democratic Sen. Daniel Patrick Moynihan and then-Senate Majority

Leader Bob Dole, a Kansas Republican, when the U.S. Senate dedicated the Italian white marble bust of former vice president Spiro Agnew just outside the Senate chamber. Under an 1886 Senate resolution, all vice presidents, whose only constitutional function is to serve as president of the Senate, are to be honored with a bust placed in the Capitol. But when it came to honoring Agnew, the nation's 31st vice president, there were many who said he didn't deserve such a high tribute. After all, they argued, Agnew resigned his high office in 1973 after pleading no contest to charges of tax evasion stemming from a contract kickback scheme dating back to the 1960s, when he was Maryland governor. He paid a $10,000 fine and served no jail time. And from then on he lived in virtual anonymity and disgrace, mostly in Ocean City, Md. and Palm Springs, Calif., until his death in 1996. But supporters fought for his bust's inclusion in the vice presidential pantheon since he did serve as vice president, and since his alleged crimes stemmed from a time when he was not in that office. Agnew backers won the battle and a dedication ceremony, attended by Agnew, then 76, and his wife Judy, was held on May 24, 1995, more than 22 years after he left office and a year before he died..

I covered that ceremony and wrote this in a column for the *Gannett News Service:*

> "Now many might think it a stretch trying to come up with something nice to say about Agnew, the steel-edged son of Greek immigrants who carved out a reputation as Richard Nixon's mean-spirited hatchet man, and is often recalled for his widely quoted alliterative attacks on the news media. Remember 'nattering nabobs of negativism?'
>
> "But Senate Majority Leader Bob Dole had no trouble at all. With Memorial Day upon us, he chose to focus on Agnew's meritorious military service in World War II - Army captain, company commander and Bronze Star winner in the 10th Armored Division that saw combat in France and Germany. Dole, a decorated World War II veteran himself, also emotionally recalled Agnew's steadfast defense as vice president of the millions of men and women serving in the U.S. armed forces during the divisive Vietnam War.
>
> " 'During a time when many believed that patriotism and military service were something to ridicule, Ted Agnew ... with strong words, left no doubt where he stood,' Dole said. 'Millions of Americans were proud to stand with him.'

"An Army honor guard stood at attention behind Dole as he spoke. "Agnew left no doubt where he stood in those dark Vietnam days. He wrote in his autobiography in 1980 that he was 'enraged' when he saw on TV 'a scruffy gang of characters' carrying a Viet Cong flag down Pennsylvania Avenue. He railed at the TV networks for treating the incident as just another expression of dissent. To Agnew, carrying the enemy flag was treason, and he said so.

"But most of all, he wasn't willing to take lying down the vitriolic epithets - 'baby killers' and the like - being hurled at American servicemen and women serving loyally in Vietnam. So being an old Army man, he proudly defended his own, taking on anti-war protesters at every turn.

" 'A spirit of national masochism prevails, encouraged by an effete corps of impudent snobs who characterize themselves as intellectuals,' Agnew sneered in an October 1969 speech in New Orleans."

But now, I noted in the column, we had come 26 years since those stormy days. Agnew was older, thinner and considerably more mellow when he showed up at the dedication ceremony. However, he still had that great tan and the slicked-back silver hair that were his trademarks . He acknowledged the controversy and awkwardness of the occasion in his speech.

"I am not blind and deaf to the fact that many people feel that this is a ceremony that should not take place," he said in a voice far less strident than it was some two decades past. "Regardless of their personal view of me, this ceremony has less to do with Spiro Agnew than with the office I held."

He offered a spirited defense of the much-maligned American vice presidency, which he said had long been a target for ridicule by everyone from TV comics to vice presidents themselves.

Later, examining the bust unveiled by his wife, Agnew displayed a sense of humor he rarely showed as vice president. He said the sculptor had done a "superlative job" of capturing in marble what one writer called his "squinty little eyes."

Moynihan was the only Democrat to speak. He volunteered because no other Senate Democrat wanted to be tainted by having to say something nice about the disgraced Agnew. And Moynihan had more reason than most to not speak. Back in the late 1960s, when Moynihan was assistant to Republican President Richard Nixon and directing the White House office on Urban Affairs, Agnew went out and undercut his welfare reform plan within the administration and among some Republican members of Congress. Moynihan's plan never made it, due in large part to Agnew's opposition. Nonetheless, he spoke on behalf of the Democrats. A *Gannett News Service* dispatch said Moynihan "hailed Agnew as a 'new breed' of politician who found 'the pulse of middle America.'" Moynihan went on to say, "In a tempestuous time, he (Agnew) was a strong partisan voice." Hardly lavish praise. But being a politician himself, Moynihan was willing to give the man his due.

Stephen Hess, a Brookings Institution political scholar and deputy to Moynihan in the Nixon White House, said the gesture was typical of the late New York senator, a magnanimous man who seldom bore grudges. "There was no love lost between Moynihan and Agnew, but his appearance there showed his generosity of spirit," Hess said.

One vice president who seldom got a fair shake, especially from the news media, was Dan Quayle, the 41-year-old, youthful-looking Indiana senator tapped by Republican George H.W. Bush to be his running mate in 1988. For the most part, Quayle was covered by the news media as a running joke, no matter what he said or did. He will forever be remembered by the public for misspelling "potato," and not much else, despite some solid work and accomplishments in foreign and domestic affairs both as senator and vice president.

For example, he co-authored with Democratic Sen. Edward Kennedy, of Massachusetts, the 1982 Job Training Partnership Act, which has trained millions of low-income and low-skilled young people for better-paying jobs.

Quayle got himself off on the wrong foot when the elder Bush introduced him as his surprise vice presidential pick under the hot August sun in New Orleans' Spanish Plaza on the second day of the 1988 Republican National Convention being held there. Quayle, who only 90 minutes before had been told he was the choice, ripped off his suit jacket, bounded up on the stage, punched the flabbergasted Bush on the arm, pulled him close and shouted with the thrust of a fist, "Let's go get 'em!"

The TV networks played that scene to the hilt, over and over, depicting Quayle as a wet-behind-the-ears hick who had no business sitting a heartbeat away from the presidency. I was there for that scene and I often told friends that Quayle looked like "an excited puppy wetting all over the rug at the sight of his family returning home." Quayle, in his memoir, "Standing Firm," wrote, "I looked like the guy on a game show who just won the Oldsmobile." We can only speculate how he would have been covered had he not done that.

But that was just the beginning. The following day, Quayle was immersed in a full-fledged controversy. Political opponents charged that he used family influence to join the Indiana National Guard in 1969 as a way of avoiding service in Vietnam. Quayle repeatedly denied the charge, and no solid evidence to the contrary was ever produced. But it did not go away. Almost immediately, the convention hall, Louisiana's now-infamous Superdome, was abuzz with rumors that Quayle would be dropped from the ticket by Bush. He wasn't, of course, and went on the become the nation's 37th vice president. But he was irreparably damaged in the eyes of most Democrats and the news media. I wrote my share of stories about Quayle messing up, but never maliciously and always in a way that I thought was fair. Others were not so careful. And the TV comics never let up. Some of the jokes were cute, but many were mean. Through it all, Quayle was always polite, never took cheap shots back at his critics and managed to maintain an optimistic outlook, even though it deeply hurt his children to have their father the object of such sharply barbed ridicule. Writing in "Standing Firm," Quayle said his son Tucker, then a high school freshman, was the self-appointed family monitor of Quayle jokes on TV, "telling us at breakfast which ones were actually funny and dismissing the ones that just seemed stupid or mean-spirited."

I did try to set the Quayle record straight back in May 1992 - a task which reporters are supposed perform as a matter of routine, but sometimes do not. It came after Quayle made his "Murphy Brown" speech in San Francisco. That was the speech in which Quayle set out to highlight the importance of a nuclear family that has a mother and a father. In his address, to underscore the point, he criticized then-popular fictional TV character Murphy Brown, a television reporter played with considerable panache by Candice Bergen. Brown, as part of the show's story line, had chosen to have a child out of wedlock and raise it alone. Quayle tried to use it as an illustration of how the popular media were extolling alternative lifestyles and sending the wrong message to a vulnerable, youthful public. Here is what he said in the speech:

"Bearing babies irresponsibly is, simply, wrong. Failing to support children one has fathered is wrong. We must be unequivocal about this.

"It doesn't help matters when prime-time TV has Murphy Brown - a character who supposedly epitomizes today's intelligent, highly paid, professional woman - mocking the importance of fathers by bearing a child alone and calling it just another 'lifestyle choice.' "

Hollywood, media and political reaction was swift. Most of it was negative, largely denouncing Quayle for what critics saw as a vicious attack on all single mothers, which it was not. Murphy Brown used her show opening the fall 1992 season to lampoon Quayle and his stand. But despite the furor, all he was saying was that "two parents, married to each other, are better in most cases for children than one." Note that he said "most cases," a notion that many people agree with.

Here is part of what I wrote offering another perspective on the Quayle speech in a May 1992 column for the *Gannett News Service*:

> "Quayle's knock on fictional TV reporter Murphy Brown for bearing a baby out of wedlock and making light of it was viewed by many aging baby boomers who have risen to positions of responsibility and power in newsrooms around the country as a direct attack on them.
>
> "After all, Murphy Brown is them, even if most of them aren't choosing to have children without the benefit of marriage.
>
> "Like many editors and reporters at the national level, Brown is fortyish, bright, college-educated, sophisticated, well-traveled and has a bit of an attitude.
>
> "Also, like many of them, she came of age during the Vietnam war, is still politically liberal, continues to be irreverent toward most institutions and, thanks to Watergate, remains somewhat distrustful of government and those in positions of authority.
>
> "And, she takes a certain swaggering glee in trashing those she doesn't agree with, much as her real-life counterparts in the news media do.
>
> "But woe to anyone who has the temerity to trash Murphy, or her media admirers. Then, it's all-out war. Therefore, when a conservative baby boomer such as Quayle - symbol of all the Murphy Browns disdain - came along and punched Murphy in the nose, it hurt twice as much. It was viewed as akin to getting beat up by the neighborhood nerd."

That column touched a nerve in many readers. I received 42 letters on it, more than for any piece I had written before or since. All but two were in support of Quayle and basically said they not only agreed with what he had to say, but also cheered my putdown of the media's response to him.

Eventually, long after the furor died down and the Bush-Quayle team lost its re-election bid, several prominent Democrats, including former President Bill Clinton and former New York Gov. Mario Cuomo, came around to admitting that Quayle's message was on the right track.

Clinton, in a 1995 presidential speech at the University of Texas in Austin said, "The single biggest social problem in our society may be the growing absence of fathers from their children's homes, because it contributes to so many other social problems. One child in four grows up in a fatherless home. Without a father to help guide, without a father to care, without a father to teach boys to be men and to teach girls to expect respect from men, it's harder."

Those words were not much different from what Quayle said three years earlier, but they evoked hardly a whimper of protest. Either Quayle was ahead of his time, or the media didn't like the messenger.

Said Quayle in a 1996 interview with me, "Bill Clinton was at the time leading the charge and being critical of me. Now he gives my speech. That shows how far we've come. And that's important to have everyone focusing on the family, communities, neighborhoods. To this day I still don't understand the controversy."

Politics, Baseball,
Movies Stars and War Do Mix

.

Thanks to my eventually becoming a White House correspondent for USA TODAY, I got to meet "The Great DiMaggio," as Ernest Hemingway referred to the Yankee Clipper in his novel "The Old Man and the Sea." Joe DiMaggio was a boyhood hero and near-god in the Italian-American community of Utica, N.Y., where I grew up.

His importance to the Italian immigrants who lived there, and their sons and daughters being raised as new Americans, went far beyond his talents and accomplishments as a slugging center fielder for the New York Yankees. He was one of the first Italian-Americans to make it to the top in the high-profile world of American popular culture. (Frank Sinatra came a few years later.) DiMaggio was living proof that the American Dream, which Italian immigrants in the early 1900s so innocently and fervently embraced, was not just a myth. If at the height of the Great Depression the son of a humble Italian fisherman from San Francisco could become respected and revered, so could their children. And they could do it as he did, with style, grace and quiet dignity.

But while he always remained intensely private, DiMaggio knew how important an icon he was, not only to Italian-Americans, but also to all American youth.

Pictures of "Joe D" — as he was respectfully referred to in East Utica — hung in barbershops, grocery stores, pool halls, restaurants, shoemaker shops and laundries, often next to portraits of Franklin Roosevelt and Jesus, and usually in more prominent positions than the other two.

When DiMaggio came to the Yankees in 1936, few Italian immigrants knew much about baseball, let alone its intricate rules, statistics and strategies. But they surely knew who he was. And many became automatic and deeply loyal Yankees fans because of him.

"How did the Yanks make out?" my grandfather would ask every afternoon.

But DiMaggio's appeal was not limited to Italian-Americans. He was adopted as a role model by millions of kids across the country. Al Gore, while running for president in 1988, told me that when he was growing up DiMaggio was one of his heroes, too.

I got to meet DiMaggio long after my boyhood had passed. It was on July 9, 1991. I had just turned 50 three days before. President George H.W. Bush invited him to the White House along with Boston Red Sox legend Ted Williams to mark the 50th anniversary of two of the greatest feats in baseball history - DiMaggio's 56-consecutive-game hitting streak, a record that still stands, and Williams' .406 batting average, the last major leaguer to hit over .400. Both records were set in 1941, the year I was born. Bush, who said he was 17 in 1941, honored the two Hall of Famers in a Rose Garden ceremony on the day of the All-Star Game, being held at the Sky Dome in Toronto that year. Bush said DiMaggio, then 76, "bespoke excellence." And he viewed Williams, then 72, as "John Wayne in a Red Sox uniform."

After the ceremony, the trio went to the South Lawn, boarded Marine One, the presidential helicopter, and flew off to Andrews Air Force Base in suburban Maryland where Air Force One is billeted. They then got on the presidential aircraft and flew to Toronto for the All-Star Game. But before they left, I got my chance to meet The Yankee Clipper. Just as the Rose Garden ceremony ended, I dashed under the rope corralling the press corps, and mixing in quickly with the invited guests, ran up to DiMaggio. I stammered out who I was and asked him for his autograph, thrusting a blank sheet of paper at him. He cordially signed and shook my hand. I then looked toward Williams, figuring I could pull off a doubleheader. But it was too late. He was already on his way into the Oval Office. What I remember most about Williams was his little speech. He excused himself for not being much of speechmaker and then gave one of the most eloquent expressions of thanks I ever heard. He said he considered himself a lucky man because he got to do in his lifetime the two things he loved best - playing baseball and serving his country.

We all know what Williams accomplished on the baseball field. But what many don't know is that he was a Marine Corps pilot during World War II and the Korean War, interrupting his baseball career twice to answer the call. And unlike DiMaggio, whose Army service in World War II was largely limited to playing baseball and entertaining the troops, Williams flew 39 combat missions in Korea and compiled a military record not as impressive as his baseball accomplishments, but nonetheless, exemplary. He flew in the same fighter-jet squadron as Marine pilot John Glenn, who went on to become an astronaut, the first American to orbit the Earth and a Democratic senator from Ohio.

Williams, a loyal Republican, was a close friend of the elder Bush. Not only were they both pilots in the Naval service (the Marine Corps is part of the Navy) during World War II, they both were avid fishermen. In January 1989, when Bush was president-elect, Williams and he went bonefishing in Islamorada, in the Florida Keys. It was one week before the inauguration, Bush's last chance to relax before taking over the awesome duties of the presidency. His choosing of Williams to be one of his fishing partners was a testament to their friendship.

During the 1990s, Williams suffered a series of strokes. But he never lost his fighting spirit. Despite his illness, he showed up on several occasions to campaign on behalf of his friend's son, George W. Bush. One such time was in January 1999, when the younger Bush was seeking the 2000 Republican presidential nomination. Williams was a guest of honor at the annual baseball dinner in Manchester, N.H., a charity event attended by major leaguers and former major leaguers who live in the New England area. With New Hampshire being a key presidential primary state, and the vote a year away, the younger Bush showed up at the party and gained the public endorsement of Williams, who made his speech from a wheelchair. I again tried to get his autograph, but the crowd of kids around him was too thick. I didn't have the heart to muscle my way to the front. Bush, then governor of Texas and a former part-owner of the Texas Rangers baseball team, wove his way through the dinner crowd handing out replica baseball cards with his picture on the front and his political record on the back - a clever campaigning tool. But neither the cards nor the Williams endorsement did him enough good with Republican primary voters in New Hampshire. He got trounced by Arizona Sen. John McCain. Bush did, however, come back and win New Hampshire in the 2000 general election, narrowly beating Democrat Al Gore. Yet in 2004, New Hampshire spurned Bush again and went for Democrat John Kerry, from neighboring Massachusetts.

Less than two months after the younger Bush took office in January 2001, he invited all of the living members of Baseball's Hall of Fame to the White House for a luncheon to mark the opening of the baseball season, a season that would end in sadness a little more than a month after the September 11 attacks on New York and Washington. But that spring day at the White House was a festive one as the great players and their wives assembled in the crystal-chandeliered splendor of the East Room. Williams, who was ill at the time, did not attend. He would die a little more than a year later, at age 83. Standing in the back of the room with the rest of my fellow White House reporters, I heard the familiar voice of Phil Rizzuto, "The Scooter," the former Yankee shortstop and announcer. "Wow! Cora.! Look!" he said in awe as he gazed around the storied room. "It's the White House!" It was genuine Rizzuto, who by then was in his 80s, but had never lost his innocent sense of boyish wonder.

Bush spoke with the likes of Stan Musial, Hank Aaron, Reggie Jackson, Nolan Ryan, Sandy Koufax, Al Kaline and Carl Yastrezemski arrayed behind him. And there, standing to the left of the president, looking very solemn, was Yogi Berra. I had brought my camera with me and stood in back snapping away, feeling like a kid in a candy shop. Then a wild idea came to me: "Wouldn't it be great if I could get a picture of Yogi, the president and me?" But I dismissed the thought as quick as it came to me. I could never pull it off. The Secret Service wouldn't allow it. But when the ceremony ended and Bush turned to start mingling with the players, some hidden force took hold and propelled me to the front of the room where Bush was talking to Berra. "Mr. President," I interrupted. "Would you take a picture with me and Yogi?" Gordon Johndroe, a Bush aide, took my camera and the three of us posed. The picture is one of my most cherished mementoes - Yogi in the center, the president and me standing on either side of him. Just as the camera flashed, a strong hand grabbed my arm and a burly Secret Service agent escorted me back to the press position. But I got my prize.

A few sports stars parlayed their athletic heroics into solid political careers: Hall of Fame pitcher Jim Bunning is now a Kentucky U.S. senator. Olympic track star Jim Ryun is a congressman from Kansas. Former St Louis Cardinals pitcher Wilmer "Vinegar Bend" Mizell, of North Carolina, served in the U.S. House from 1969-75. Former Buffalo Bills quarterback Jack Kemp represented Western New York in the House of Representatives from 1971-1989. He ran for president in 1988 and for vice president in 1996. All were Republicans.

One Democratic athlete-turned-politician ran for president in 2000. That was former New York Knicks basketball star Bill Bradley, then a retired senator from New Jersey. Bradley's run in the Democratic presidential primaries against Vice President Al Gore lacked the kind of spark upon which successful national campaigns are built. And although he came within four percentage points of beating the heavily favored Gore in New Hampshire, he never won anywhere and gracefully dropped out a month later. But one thing I always will remember from the Bradley campaign is how big a man he really was. As he traveled the country in search of votes, he often visited inner-city high schools in gritty neighborhoods carrying an important message to the young people who packed the gymnasiums to hear the former NBA star: Stay in school, work hard, make your families proud and never give up.

It was hardly the kind of message that would gain him votes. Besides, few if any of these kids were old enough to vote. But he cared about them. If he didn't, he wouldn't have gone in the first place. You could see his words, delivered in a low-key, somewhat shy manner, striking a chord with many of the mostly black kids in the bleachers. There was no snickering or horseplay from the students, who can have a way of being rowdy when politicians come to call. With Bradley, they would sit silently in rapt attention. After all, here was a Rhodes Scholar who also was a real basketball player, one who had played his way to the very top of the professional ranks, telling them that school was important. He would urge them to work hard and try to succeed not only for their own sake, but also for the pride of their parents and families who were pulling for them and counting heavily on their children doing better than they did. Then, Bradley would change into his sweats and play basketball with the boys and girls on the school teams. It was a great show and made good TV, which I am sure Bradley had in mind when staging the events. But the message was sincere. You can't fake that.

Another example of Bradley's solid character was demonstrated on a campaign stop in Stratham, N.H. After he finished speaking, a teenage boy pushed his way through the crowd toward the candidate and shyly asked him to autograph a shiny, orange basketball. Bradley aides tried to muscle the boy away, but the candidate waved them off. Taking out a felt-tip pen, he autographed the ball in large, deliberate letters and asked to whom it should be inscribed. "My friend in the hospital," the boy almost whispered. "What's his name?" Bradley asked. The boy told him. Bradley wrote, "To Tom." Then the candidate asked a third question. "Do you want me to write, 'Get well soon?" "Yes, sir," the boy thankfully replied. No big deal, some might say. Stars do that all the time. Some do, some don't. But looking in on this scene, it was easy to see that Bradley did it not out of obligation, but out of courtesy and kindness.

Like athletes who turned their on-the-field achievements into political fame, there are many bona fide war heroes who did the same. George Washington was our first in a long, proud line of decorated war heroes who went on to highly successful political careers: Early war-hero presidents included Andrew Jackson, William Henry Harrison, Zachary Taylor, Ulysses S. Grant, William McKinley and Teddy Roosevelt. More recent war heroes include Dwight Eisenhower, John F. Kennedy and George H.W. Bush. At age 19, the elder Bush was the youngest Navy pilot to serve in World War II.

Bob Dole, the former Republican Kansas senator and Senate majority leader, entered politics after World War II. As a young Army lieutenant he suffered crippling wounds in fierce fighting in the mountains of Italy. He permanently lost the use of one arm in that battle. Dole ran twice for president, in 1988 and again in 1996, winning the GOP nomination in '96 but losing to Bill Clinton. He also was Gerald Ford's vice presidential running mate in 1986. Sine his political retirement in 1996, Dole has been a tireless campaigner for veterans' causes and led the fundraising effort to build the World War II Memorial in Washington, D.C., dedicated in 2004, nearly 60 years after the end of that bloody war. Known for his often-gruff demeanor, Dole's eyes well up with tears whenever he talks about the sacrifices made by veterans.

There have been several presidential elections where a candidate's war service, or lack thereof, became an issue in the campaign. In 1988, Republican vice presidential candidate Dan Quayle was charged with pulling family strings to join the Indiana National Guard and avoid service in Vietnam. Bill Clinton had to deal with charges in 1992 that he evaded the draft to stay out of military service during the Vietnam war. In both cases, the candidates won the elections they were running in, despite the charges.

In 2000, and again in 2004, George W. Bush was accused of not only using family influence to join the Texas Air National Guard and avoid

Vietnam service, but also of being Absent Without Leave in the final year of his hitch. The issue reached the peak of its intensity in September 2004 when CBS-TV was accused of airing falsified documents lending credence to the charges against Bush. The ensuing controversy led to the early retirement of veteran CBS anchorman Dan Rather.

At the same time, Democratic presidential candidate John Kerry, who had chosen to make his service as a Navy Swift Boat officer in Vietnam a key centerpiece in his campaign, came under attack from the so-called Swift Boat Veterans for Truth, a Republican-funded advocacy group that included several veterans who had served with Kerry. They charged that the Massachusetts senator had exaggerated his war record and betrayed his comrades after leaving the Navy by opposing the war and accusing them of war crimes. The Bush-Kerry military service debate raged on without resolution through to the final days of the 2004 election, which Bush won, 51 percent to 48 percent.

Bob Kerrey, the former Nebraska Democratic governor and senator was the first Vietnam war hero to try his hand at running for president in 1992. But after a lackluster campaign in the early primary states, he dropped out.

In 1969, Kerrey was a young Navy lieutenant serving in the SEALS, an elite outfit charged with undertaking dangerous clandestine missions. He won the Medal of Honor, the nation's highest military decoration, for "conspicuous gallantry" in the face of enemy fire as leader of a SEALS assault team. His Navy citation said Kerrey, who lost the lower part of one leg in the assault, "received massive injuries from a grenade which exploded at his feet and threw him backward onto the jagged rocks. Although bleeding profusely and suffering great pain, he displayed outstanding courage and presence of mind in immediately directing his element's fire into the heart of the enemy camp. Utilizing his radio, Lt. (jg.) Kerrey called in the second element's fire support which caught the confused Viet Cong in a devastating crossfire. After successfully suppressing the enemy's fire, and although immobilized by his multiple wounds, he continued to maintain calm, superlative control as he ordered his team to secure and defend an extraction site."

Kerrey, while governor of Nebraska nearly two decades later, made the gossip columns when he dated actress Debra Winger. But politics has an uncanny way of humbling the mighty. Kerrey knows it all too well.

Back in January 1992, while serving as a Nebraska senator, he found it out the hard way while campaigning for the Democratic presidential nomination in the harsh, snowy winter of New Hampshire. One bitter cold night, Kerrey, with me in tow, stopped at an isolated farmhouse to engage in what has become a time-honored part of New Hampshire campaigning - sitting down for coffee with a living room full of neighbors. It is seen and widely praised as the last chance presidential candidates get to meet and talk to real people before the campaign turns to less-personal barnstorming rallies and highly scripted TV spots.

When we walked into the farmhouse through the side door, which brought us into the kitchen, we encountered a homespun scene: children sitting around the table coloring with crayons while a mother supervised and told them to shush. This way, their parents could gather in the living room and listen to Kerrey without interruption by the kids. Or so they thought.

Kerrey entered the living room. A group of about 12 adults, most casually dressed in jeans and flannel shirts, stood up. He shook hands all around and urged them to sit down. But rather than pull up a folding chair, sit among them and chat in the spirit of informality these events are designed for, Kerrey chose to stand and speak. He positioned himself between two doors - one leading from the kitchen, to his right, the other leading to a bathroom, to his left.

A minute into his speech, a little boy came in from the kitchen, crossed in front of Kerrey, entered the bathroom and closed the door. Kerrey was unruffled. He continued his speech, which had a tone much more formal than the occasion merited. The subject was health care. A few seconds later, the toilet flushed and out came the little boy, who crossed in front of Kerrey again to get back to the kitchen. Kerrey kept talking, only to have his stage crossed again, this time by a little girl. She went into the bathroom and repeated the ritual: close the door, flush the toilet, cross back in front of Kerrey and return to the kitchen. Some parents in the audience, I assumed the ones with the children who had weak bladders, tittered nervously. But Kerrey pressed on through three or four more kiddie trips to the bathroom, pausing to remark at one point, "Boy, that is a popular room."

Panned by some critics as cold and aloof, Kerry finished a distant third in New Hampshire to Massachusetts Sen. Paul Tsongas and Arkansas

Gov. Bill Clinton. Clinton used that second-place finish to declare himself the "Comeback Kid" after being hit by charges of draft evasion and an affair with singer Gennifer Flowers. Kerrey went on to win the South Dakota primary, his only victory, and dropped out of the race by early March. He never tried to run for president again. Now retired from politics, Kerrey is president of The New School, a progressive liberal arts university in New York City.

Comedian Bob Hope, a staunch Republican, generously entertained American troops at war over a 50-year period that began with World War II and ended with the Persian Gulf War. Had he been alive during the Iraq War, you could rest assured that he would have been there, too. My one personal encounter with Hope came during the 1988 presidential campaign when he hosted a $5,000-a-couple fundraiser for then-Vice President George H.W. Bush and wife Barbara at his elegant Tudor mansion in Toluca Lake, near Hollywood. As a member of the press pool following Bush on the campaign trail, we motorcaded to the Hope mansion, passed through the guarded, high iron gates and parked in the long oval driveway. The usual drill for fundraisers in private homes is that they are closed to the press and we wait outside in the vans until they are over.

But this time, shortly after the Bushes went in, a white-jacketed steward came out to the vans and said, "Mr. Hope would like you to come in as his guests." We were shocked, but gladly accepted under the ground rule that no TV or still cameras would be allowed. Walking through to the party, which was being held out on the torchlit terrace and around the pool, Hope quickly came over, bid us welcome and told us to enjoy ourselves. Which we did, although, for a bunch of hard-charging reporters, I have to admit we were less than our usual aggressive, confident selves. We were dazzled by the magnitude of the stars we saw, most of them from Hollywood's Golden Age of the Thirites and Forties: the James Stewarts, the Fred McMurrays, Glenn Ford, Anne Jeffries, Gene Autry, Virginia Mayo, Pat Boone and more-recent luminaries such as Lee Majors, Cheryl Ladd and Jaclyn Smith. I remember them as being elegantly dressed, very polite and highly interested in talking to us about our jobs and the campaign. It was a memorable moment I never would have experienced if I were not a political reporter. I often tell people that I once attended a party at Bob Hope's home. Many think it is a bigger deal than going to a party at the White House.

When my non-political friends and relatives talk to me about my coverage of national politicians, and my personal encounters with them, they rarely ask where he or she stands on health care or taxes. Instead, they ask, 'What are they really like?" "What are my personal impressions of them?" "What do I know about them that isn't being reported, can't be reported or that will give a better insight into their character?" So I figured that if that's what my friends and relatives ask me, it is what strangers around the country who live outside the Washington Beltway would ask me, too.

While covering the 1988 presidential campaign, I figured that one way to learn a lot about candidates was to ask them who their boyhood heroes were. The answers were illuminating.

Delaware Democratic Sen. Joe Biden told me his hero was an uncle he never knew other than through a picture of a soldier in uniform that held a prominent place in his living room. The uncle, his mother's brother, was killed in World War II, when Biden was too young to have known him. But he was his hero and role model, nonetheless.

Gary Hart, the enigmatic 1988 Democratic presidential frontrunner at the time of our interview, could not recall having any boyhood heroes. Only two months after our interview, he was caught by reporters from the *Miami Herald* spending the night in a Washington town house with model Donna Rice, an attractive young woman who was not his wife. It destroyed his campaign and his hopes of ever becoming president. But I always felt, even when everyone was predicting that Hart would be the next occupant of the Oval Office, that the man would never catch on with the American public once they got to know him better or realize that they could not know him better. Americans want to know who their presidents are. Unlike Hart, who thought there were certain areas of privacy that he could maintain for himself, Americans have to reach a comfort level with their president, a level that transcends partisan politics. When they don't find it, they move on. I believe that would have eventually happened with Hart, regardless of the Donna Rice affair.

My interview with Hart came during a late-March 1987 campaign swing through South Dakota and Iowa, prior to his official announcement of candidacy on April 9 at Red Rocks National Park near Denver. Our encounter took place in a car driven by a campaign worker as we traveled from one stop to the next near Des Moines. He preferred to do it that way rather than sit down in a room and talk face to face. In the car, Hart sat in the front seat and I sat in the back. I asked my questions and he answered, seldom turning back to look at me as he spoke. When I asked him who his heroes were, he quickly ticked off the usual Thomas Jefferson, John F. Kennedy, Franklin Roosevelt mantra that many politicians safely slip into when asked such questions. I said, "No, not your political heroes. Who were your boyhood heroes, people you admired growing up?" Hart was silent. I waited. No answer. I tried to prod him. I knew he had grown up in Joplin, Mo. I knew Joplin was the first city where New York Yankee great Mickey Mantle played minor league baseball before moving up to the majors. I asked if he had ever seen Mantle play. He said he didn't recall, but did remember going to a Joplin game with his father. I could tell he was not very comfortable talking about his personal life. He would rather talk about education policy, relations with the Soviet Union. Still, he gave no answer for his hero. I decided to wait him out. After about a minute, which seemed like an hour, Hart broke the silence. "Let the record show that I am cogitating on that," he said. He never returned to the question.

Michael Dukakis, the bushy-browed Massachusetts governor who eventually became the Democratic presidential nominee in 1988, projected a far friendlier and easy-going persona in our 1987 interview than he ever showed during his '88 campaign. Our talk took place on the US Airways Shuttle between Washington and Boston. Politicians are busy people. Dukakis was harder-working than most and very earnest. He had little time to waste. So he had his staff book our interview for his flight home to Boston after meetings in Washington. I bought a round-trip ticket, conducted the interview on the 90-minute flight to Boston, finished when we landed, thanked him for his time and turned around and flew back to Washington on the next plane. I never left Boston's Logan International Airport. Sometimes you have to go to such lengths to get your story.

During the interview, I asked Dukakis if he had a boyhood hero. His answer was terrific. Without missing a beat, he said as a boy he liked Phil Masi, a journeyman catcher who played from 1939-49 for the Boston Braves and finished his 13-year career in 1952 with the Chicago White Sox. I remembered my Phil Masi baseball card well, a craggy-faced, bowling ball of a man. It was an odd choice when in those late-40s days Boston was packed with stars such as Ted Williams, Dom DiMaggio, Johnny Pesky and Bobby Doerr of the Red Sox and Warren Spahn and

Johnny Sain pitching for the Braves. I asked Dukakis why the obscure and unheralded Masi? Without hesitation he said, "He was a short, stocky catcher and he was tough. I was a short, stocky catcher when I was a kid, too. I liked him. He played his heart out." It was so in character with Dukakis - no flash, no dash, just admiration for people who work hard at their jobs and keep plugging away. People can identify with that. It said a lot about the candidate.

So you can imagine my surprise when some 18 months later, in his third presidential debate with George H.W. Bush, Dukakis was asked by ABC's Ann Compton who he would hold up as heroes for young people today. I sat there in shock in the Pauley Pavilion on the campus of UCLA, when Dukakis, rather than throw Phil Masi in with some prominent Americans, stammered a bit and blandly answered, "Well, when I think of heroes, I think back, not presently, Ann. But there are many people who I admire in this country today. Some of them are in public life in the Senate, the Congress. Some of my fellow governors who are real heroes to me. I think of those young athletes who represented us at the Olympics were tremendously impressive….." He went on to throw in Jonas Salk, the scientist who created the polio vaccine, the clergy, drug counselors and community volunteers. All politically correct, respectable answers. But no Phil Masi. The windy Dukakis response might have been a good civics answer, but it did nothing to humanize the candidate. It only reinforced the already widespread notion that he was humorless, cold and wooden.

It was in this same debate that Dukakis, an opponent of the death penalty, was asked by CNN's Bernard Shaw if he would favor imposing capital punishment if his wife, Kitty, had been raped and murdered. The audience gasped at the personal and brutal nature of the question. But without emotion, Dukakis launched into his stock answer. "No, I don't, Bernard. And I think you know that I've opposed the death penalty during all of my life. I don't see any evidence that it's a deterrent, and I think there are better and more effective ways to deal with violent crime…."

Looking for a human side of Dukakis in that debate, many onlookers found none. It was there, but he refused to let it show.

President George W. Bush press conference in the White House Rose Garden. Oct. 4, 2005. The author is in the front row, right. (White House photo)

FLIGHT CERTIFICATE

This is to certify that
Richard Benedetto
has flown aboard Air Force One as a guest of George Bush,
President of the United States of America.

September 27, 1990

Presidential Aircraft Commander

Proof that I flew on Air Force One as a guest of President George H.W. Bush in 1990, shortly after the current 747 version of the aircraft was put into service. It does not say that USA TODAY paid for the trip, and many others.

Interview with Vice President Al Gore aboard Air Force Two after we had inspected flood damage in California, Idaho and Washington state. January, 1997. (White House photo)

113

Meeting with President Bill Clinton in the Oval Office. Clinton, recovering from a knee injury, was still wearing a cast. June 1997. (White House photo)

With First Lady Hillary Rodham Clinton at tour of the ancient Indian cliff dwellings, Mesa Verde, Colo. May 1999. (White House photo)

GEORGE BUSH

June 7, 2001

Dear Richard,

Barbara and I love the book you sent. How thoughtful
of you.

We moved our base to Kennebunkport about three
weeks ago. Heaven!!

We all rest easier knowing that you and No. 43 "have
Washington under control." Keep up the good work!

All the best,

Mr. Richard Benedetto
USA Today
1000 Wilson Boulevard
Arlington, VA 22229

WALKER'S POINT, POST OFFICE BOX 492, KENNEBUNKPORT, MAINE 04046

Thank-you letter from George H.W. Bush sent after I mailed him a
book of coastal Maine illustrations. June 2001, more than eight years
after he left office.

Interviewing President George W. Bush aboard Air Force One. Judy Keen of USA TODAY is to my left. Note that Bush is holding our tape recorders for easier voice pickup. August 2004. (White House photo)

Oval Office interview with President George W. Bush shortly before his second inauguration. Judy Keen of USA TODAY is on the left. January 2005. (White House photo)

Jogging with President George H.W. Bush at
Kennebunkport, Me., May 1989. (Ron Edmonds photo)

Jogging With "41"

The first President Bush had a reputation for being a nice guy, but somewhat out of touch with the American people. His blueblood background - son of a Wall Street investment banker, brought up in the toney New York City suburb of Greenwich, Conn., educated at the oh-so-proper Andover Academy in New England and later at his father's alma mater, Yale University - forever cast him as a man of privilege, which he was.

From time to time he would try to convince people that he was just plain folks and not the preppy WASP everyone figured him for. He loved to talk about how he and his wife Barbara, fresh out of college, packed up their maroon 1947 Studebaker and moved to Odessa, Texas to try their luck in the oil business. He would tell with a slight stammer and a hint of a blush about how they lived in a long, narrow frame duplex, known in those parts as a shotgun house, which they shared with a mother-daughter team of hookers whose nightly activities could be heard through the paper-thin walls. He would wax on about his love for country music, his fondness for pork rinds, his penchant for cowboy boots. But to most, he was still the rich guy who was so isolated from the rigors of day-to-day living that he expressed astonishment when shown a price scanner at a super market checkout. (The story is not quite accurate, by the way, but it fit the public perception of Bush's image, so it was widely believed no matter how hard he protested.)

So ingrained was that rich-boy image in the public mind that when the economy went sour on his presidential watch in 1991, he not only was never able to convince the American people that he had solutions for solving the problems, but also that he even cared about their plight. It turned out to be a major factor in his defeat at the hands of two opponents - Bill Clinton and Ross Perot - who without even trying were able to exhibit a down-to-earth folksiness that in contrast only made Bush look worse. When Clinton told people he felt their pain, they believed it. When

Perot said the way to fix what was wrong with the economy was to look under the hood, roll up your sleeves and go to work, people cheered. But when Bush went out and told voters he cared, they laughed as if it was the funniest thing they ever heard. Many of the reporters who regularly covered the Bush presidency found him far more friendly and genuine than his public reputation. I got to know him better during morning jogs at Kennebunkport, where he has a summer home on the rocky Maine coast just south of Portland. Our jogging partnership began in May 1989 when Bush went up to Maine for a long weekend to meet with then-French President Francois Mitterrand. He had come to discuss the upcoming NATO summit in Brussels, which was set for the following weekend. The main topic on the agenda was arms control. The Soviet Union was still in existence then. About 100 other reporters, photographers and TV technicians had gone up from Washington with the president to cover whatever news he and Mitterrand might make.

How I came to jog with Bush is a tale of pure journalistic chutzpah. It was a Saturday morning and I was asleep in an iron-and-brass bed in the Sundial Inn, a quaint little hotel on Kennebunk Beach, about a mile from the Bush compound. From the front porch of the inn you could look to the left, on days that were not foggy, and see the Bush house about a mile north on Walker's Point, a rocky promontory that juts into the Atlantic. Offshore, a white-with-red stripe Coast Guard cutter patrolled the choppy, chilly waters to keep sightseers and fishing boats from getting too close to the presidential retreat. At 6:20 a.m. my beeper sounded, startling me awake. The message said the press pool should report immediately to cover a Bush jog at 7 a.m. The press pool is a designated group of reporters and photographers that covers presidential events when a large media entourage is unnecessary or unwieldy. Service in the pool rotates among the various news organizations. Those in the pool for a particular event report back to the others on what happened. They also share their photos and videotape.

When the signal for the pool went off, I could have turned over and gone back to sleep. I was not assigned to the pool that day. But I had never jogged with a president before, so I figured I would get into my running shoes, shorts and tee-shirt and see if they'd let me go along. It was still foggy and just starting to get light when I got into my rented car and drove to the press filing center, set up in a gymnasium at the nearby St. Anthony retreat house run by Franciscan fathers. There, the press pool was assembled and loaded into vans driven by White House staff which took us over to the Bush house. We pulled up at the gate in front of Walker Point at the stroke of 7, in time to meet the mini-motorcade of Secret Service vans taking Bush to his jogging spot. Our vans pulled in behind the group and we drove about a quarter-mile down the road and turned right onto a secluded neighborhood street.

The president, in gray sweatpants, an Oak Ridge Boys sweatshirt and blue baseball cap, jumped out of the van, followed by Millie, the First Dog, and started jogging down the street. Three Secret Service agents accompanied him - one in front, one behind and one at his side. Each carried walkie-talkies and packed handguns, although they were not visible. A police cruiser followed behind.

The press pool was ordered by the agents to take up a position on a corner Bush would pass. That way photographers could get a good angle for pictures. When the jogging party approached us, I stood in front so the president would notice my running attire. I caught the president's eye and motioned to him that I would like go along. "Come on!" he said with a wave. I stepped into the road and past the agent, and there I was, jogging side-by-side with George H. W. Bush.

We exchanged pleasantries about the beautiful weather - temperature around 60 and the orange sun rising over the blue-gray waters of the Atlantic. He asked me how far I usually jogged. I told him about three miles. He said he sticks to about half of that and said I looked like I was "keeping in good shape."

He apologized for rousting reporters so early on a Saturday morning and said it was really unnecessary for a press pool to come along because there was "no news." However, while reporters were griping about the early-morning call - some had closed down local bars the night before - they would have griped even louder if the president went jogging and didn't call. After all, something could happen. You never know.

Bush noted that he was staying on the dirt at the edge of the road because the hard pavement bothered his knees. Every so often he would call the curious Millie, who would stray off the path, back to the group.

We compared notes on local restaurants, the outcome of the Mets game the night before. He boasted about the succulence of the native lobster and discussed the golf match he played on Friday at the nearby Cape Arundel Country Club. "We lost," Bush said. "But Scowcroft is really good. He surprised me." "Scowcroft" is retired Air Force general Brent Scowcroft, who was the president's national security adviser. They became close friends, later collaborating on a book on foreign policy.

Bush, huffing and puffing, repeatedly remarked how "great" he felt being out in the early-morning air. He pointed seaward to a tiny rocky island around which the surf was splaying. "See that island over there? Covered with seals," he said. Then he pointed ahead. "You get a good view of the house from here." He meant his house.

When we circled the block and approached the press pool again, the gaggle of reporters, desperate for some news, shouted questions at the president about China, the upcoming NATO meeting and Panama, where strongman Manuel Noriega was giving the U.S. fits. One fellow reporter begged for "just one fresh quote." But the president just smiled, waved and kept running. It felt odd being on the other side of the questions. Although I had exclusive access, I didn't ask any news questions. I figured I was there at his invitation and thought it would be impolite to intrude on his privacy. But I couldn't resist asking about his Boston University commencement address he was to give the next day. He said it would be on U.S.-European relations, then still steeped in Cold War politics. Mitterrand also spoke at that graduation. I still have a tee-shirt commemorating the occasion, but it has a big coffee stain on it.

As Bush ran past the neighborhood houses, residents came out to take pictures. The president good-naturedly stopped for them and posed. At one stop, Bush took the camera from the man, handed it to me and had me take a picture of the two of them together. The fellow was most appreciative. He probably has the photo framed and hanging somewhere. How many people get to have their picture taken with the president of the United States? In jogging clothes, yet!

A Secret Service agent keeping track of the time told the president when 20 minutes were up. We actually jogged 20 minutes and 40 seconds. Bush, who by now had worked up quite a sweat, seemed relieved as he slowed to a walk. I later called Dr. Allan Cooper, an aerobics expert in Dallas. Cooper said the pattern Bush observed - 20 minutes of jogging four times a week - was ideal for building cardiovascular fitness.

As we headed back to the black suburban van that would carry the president back to his house, we shook hands and promised to do it again, which we did, several times. And it was always the same - we would talk about the weather, the baseball games of the night before, which restaurants I liked in town, how my colleagues were enjoying their stay in Kennebunkport and where they were going at night. And if there was any reporter gossip I could pass along, he eagerly gobbled it up.

But although I jogged with the president while he was vacationing in Maine, I had never jogged with him in Washington, until the fall of 1990 when one morning my office phone rang. I picked up the receiver.

"Benedetto," I said.

"Mr. Benedetto?" a very official woman's voice inquired.

"Yes," I replied.

"This is President Bush's secretary," the woman said.

I was immediately on the defensive. I have a lot of friends who like to play practical jokes and I thought this was one of them. After all, it isn't every day that the president's secretary calls.

"Yes," I said again, more than somewhat warily.

"President Bush would like to know if you would like to go jogging with him this morning," she said.

This had to be a joke. But I didn't know who could be behind it. I didn't know any women who I thought would try such a stunt. And even if it was someone put up to it by one of my male friends, why such an elaborate ruse? Their sophisticated brand of tricks ran to sending phony memos on the boss's notepaper filched from his desk or smearing your computer keyboard with sticky glue.

So I was cautious.

"When does he want to jog?" I asked.

"Could you be here at the White House at 11 a.m.?" she replied.

She sure sounded official. But if it was a joke, she probably would reveal it if I continued to play along.

"Yes, I can be there," I said.

"Good," she responded. "We'll see you at 11," and she clicked off before I could ask another question or say good-bye.

I looked at the clock. It was 9:45. If this wasn't a joke, I didn't have much time to figure it out. But I still expected someone to call or swing by my desk and begin guffawing at my gullibility. No one did.

Since I jogged at noontime just about every day, I had my running clothes at work. So I reached under my desk and grabbed my duffel bag and headed for the subway. If this is a joke, I thought, I am going to wring someone's neck.

I got off at the Farragut West station and walked two blocks, passed Lafayette Park, crossed Pennsylvania Avenue, which then was still open to auto traffic, and entered the Northwest gate of the White House. That's the gate where the press enters the heavily guarded compound.

All reporters who regularly cover the White House are issued a pass by the Secret Service, which provides it after conducting a background check, similar to the one given to employees who work on the White House staff. The picture pass, worn around the neck, has a smart chip in it so that when you enter the guardhouse you have to swipe it across a screen and punch in a four-digit PIN, which unlocks the turnstile in front of the magnetomer similar to the ones you pass through at airline security gates.

Upon entering the pressroom, which is between the West Wing, where the Oval Office is, and the White House itself, I could see that the travel pool of reporters and photographers was assembling. That meant the president was going out somewhere.

I asked what was going on, and someone said the president was going out to jog. So it wasn't a ruse after all, I thought, somewhat relieved.

I went into the men's room and changed into my running clothes and walked back out into the press room. Several of my colleagues looked at me quizzically. "I've been invited to go jogging with the president," I said.

Out on the South driveway the motorcade was assembling - presidential limousine, Secret Service communications van, vans for aides and the press and two police cruisers one for the front and one for the back of the line. The motorcade also contained a black suburban that carries a SWAT team. It has been a part of the retinue ever since John Hinckley shot President Reagan while exiting the Washington Hilton Hotel in March 1983. As I walked out, I could see the black-clad SWAT officers in their bulky bulletproof vests and carrying automatic rifles, climbing into the back of their truck.

I walked over to the press van and stood outside waiting for the president to come out of the Oval Office. In a few minutes he did, wearing his jogging clothes and accompanied by another man I did not recognize, also in jogging clothes. When they reached the limousine, the president saw me standing outside the van. I waved to him and he called me over.

"Ride with us," he said, meaning that I should ride in the big black Cadillac presidential limousine. "Wow," said one of my colleagues, wondering why I rated such special treatment.

Bush introduced me to Henry Catto, the U.S. ambassador to Britain, who was in town for a visit. Catto was an old Bush friend. A wealthy Texas businessman from San Antonio who served in several government posts in the Reagan and Bush administrations.

Bush told him that I was a regular jogging partner when we were in Kennebunkport. Catto, a distinguished looking gentleman with black hair that was graying at the temples, shook my hand. The three of us climbed into the back of the limo. Catto and the president sat on the plush black leather seats facing forward. I sat on a black leather jump seat facing them. Here we were: three men wearing tee-shirts, shorts and sneakers sitting in the back of the limousine of the president of the United States.

The motorcade pulled out of the Southwest gate and onto the city streets heading for Fort McNair, an Army base in Southeast Washington about two miles from the White House. Bush often jogged there, dating back to his days as vice president. It was secure, had a scenic route along the Anacostia River and was less intrusive on the public than running on city streets, like Bill Clinton used to do in his early years as president.

The red lights of the police cruiser at the front of the entourage were flashing and we picked up a motorcycle escort upon leaving the White House grounds. But Bush told the Secret Service agents in the limo that he wanted no sirens and that they should stop at traffic lights. An agent in the front seat relayed that presidential order into the little microphone he had attached to his sleeve near his wrist. The sirens of the motorcycles were silent in seconds.

As the presidential motorcade quietly wound its way to Fort McNair, tourists were flabbergasted to see the presidential limousine up so close and moving so slowly. Many smiled, waved and snapped pictures. Bush waved out the window on occasion, but most of the time he was prodding Catto to regale him with the latest gossip on Margaret Thatcher, who was then the British prime minister. Bush kept referring to her as "Maggie." Catto had a story about how some diplomat got sick at one of the oh-so-proper Thatcher's dinner parties, which the president found quite amusing.

When we got to the Army base, we jumped out of the car, did a few stretching exercises and began to run. Often we would encounter groups of soldiers running, all of whom in perfect cadence would give small salutes and shout, "Good Morning, Sir!" to their commander in chief. At one corner a group of jogging soldiers halted to let the presidential party pass. With a wave, Bush invited them to fall in with us. They did. As we ran, Bush asked the soldiers their names, where they were from and what they did.

As we turned a corner, a chunky fellow in blue overalls and work shirt saw us heading his way and called out, "Hiya George!"

"Hi!" Bush cheerfully called back as we passed him.

When we got out of earshot Bush chuckled and said, "That guy is quite a character. He works in maintenance and back when I was vice president he kept pestering me to have him come and play Santa Claus at one of my Christmas parties. He said he did it for other parties and would be glad to do mine. So one year I had him come over. He apparently stopped at the punch bowl a few times too often and got a little frisky with the girls, pulling them down on his lap when he handed out the gifts. Barbara didn't like it and told him. We never invited him back. What a character."

We jogged for exactly 20 minutes, which was the Bush maximum. Huffing and puffing, we headed back to the cars. When we approached the open doors of the limousine, an aide handed each of us a towel and a bottle of cold water. We climbed in and within seconds we were off.

As we pulled past the Fort McNair gate, Bush asked the driver if he would open the windows in the back so we could get some fresh air.

"We smell like goats back here," he said.

"Sorry sir," the agent said, refusing to open the windows. He had a president to protect, no matter how smelly the job.

When we got back to the White House, rather than leave the towels and plastic water bottles in the car for the Secret Service agents to pick up, Bush, like a custodian in a locker room, gathered them up in his arms and carried the bundle into the Oval Office. It was a gesture that was common in him - humble, polite to a fault and never haughty. It was a reflection of his mother's strict edict against being a bragger that he carried with him to the White House. (To illustrate the extent of that motherly influence, Bush never went to the Berlin Wall to make a speech after it fell on his watch in 1989. He said at the time that going there would look like bragging and embarrass Soviet leader Mikhail Gorbachev, with whom he was trying to build a friendly, working relationship.)

Bush always seemed to be slightly uncomfortable by the trappings of his high office and awkwardly chagrined by the public attention and adulation that went along with the job. So once he left office, he seemed more at ease with himself. I had occasion to meet up with him several times after he stepped down following his bitter defeat by Bill Clinton in 1992. Each time, he was friendly and relaxed, quick with a quip and always polite and generous. His generosity was extended to the reporters who covered him during the summer in Kennebunkport. On afternoons when he wasn't out fishing in his 24-foot cigarette boat Fidelity, he would have a Coast Guardsman on duty take reporters out for rides on the ocean - three or four at a time.

Shortly after Bush left the presidency, I interviewed him in his new office in Houston, which had a large gold-framed painting of the U.S. Capitol on the wall, rather than a picture of the White House, which one would expect. But the Capitol is significant in Bush's political life, too. He served there for four years, 1967-71, as a member of the House of Representatives from Texas. And when he was vice president, he held forth as president of the Senate for eight years, 1981-89.

But one post-presidential interview that got off to a fun start took place in Kennebunkport at the Bush home in September 1998. Bush and his former national security adviser, Brent Scowcroft, were about to publish "A World Transformed," a book on foreign policy during the Bush years that they had written together. Naturally, they were looking for some publicity, so they scheduled a round of interviews with media representatives. I got one of the first, and one of only a few actually conducted in the Bush home. The Bushes, father and son, are very careful about invitations to their homes, reserving them mostly for those they consider friends. Knowing that, I considered my invitation an honor.

I showed up for the interview at the scheduled 9 a.m. on a sunny Monday morning. I drove my rented car up to the gate house in front of the compound and told the Secret Service agent on duty I had an appointment and gave him my name. He looked at a list and asked for a photo-ID. I gave him my White House press pass, which he immediately recognized. Handing it back, he pressed a button that opened the electronic iron gate and I drove past, down a blacktop road about an eighth of a mile and then around the circular drive in front of the sprawling-yet-quaint Tudor-style Bush home. Bush and Scowcroft had just returned from playing an early-morning round of golf. Bush used to like to tee off around 6:30, when the air is crisp and the grass is heavy with dew. When he finished 18 holes, often in as little as 90 minutes, his trouser legs were usually soaking wet from about mid-calf down. Not one to stand around and chit-chat after a shot, he would jump back into the cart and zoom off after the ball. White House physician Larry Mohr, who often went along on golfing trips when Bush was president, used to refer to the breakneck speed at which the president played as "aerobic golf."

When Bush played golf as president, the press pool was allowed to go up to the first tee and watch the presidential party tee off. Reporters usually refrained from asking questions while the players were preparing to swing. One day on the golf course, a reporter overstepped the bounds and asked what the elder Bush thought of a journalist, Tadeusz Mazowiecki, becoming prime minister of Poland. Bush shook his head and grumbled under his breath, "Oh, Lord."

But Bush, while dead serious about his golf, and every other sport he took up, still liked to joke. One morning, approaching the first tee, he began speaking in the hushed tones of a TV announcer calling a golf match. Holding his clenched hand to his mouth to imitate a microphone, he whispered, "The crowd is hushed. They sense Mr. Smooth is back." Amused reporters began referring to the president as "Mr. Smooth," as in "Is Mr. Smooth playing golf today?"

Spotting my car pulling up, Bush and Scowcroft stepped toward the front door to greet me. Over to the left I saw Barbara Bush cutting some flowers in her garden. She was wearing white slacks, a green blouse and a big straw sun hat that tied under the chin. She waved and came over to say hello. After exchanging greetings and taking note of the beautiful weather, Bush, Scowcroft and I went into the house, leaving Mrs. Bush to her gardening. Inside, Bush announced that he was starving and called us into the kitchen where he put on the coffee and started making toast, two slices at a time. By the time he finished, he had created a teetering stack of crispy whole wheat bread that looked like it would tumble if one more slice were added to the pile.

When everything was ready, Bush jammed it all on a tray and carried our breakfast out into the cavernous living room filled with bookshelves, a herd of chintz-covered stuffed furniture and liberally sprinkled throughout with framed pictures of family members. Through the picture windows we could see the blue waves of the Atlantic crashing onto the rocks and sending geysers of spray into the air just 50 feet in front of us. Sitting down and balancing our coffee cups on our laps, we sipped and munched on our morning treat served by the former president. I admired the view while Bush and Scowcroft exchanged wisecracks on who played the better round of golf that day. But Bush was clearly having the most fun. He had a little tin shaker of cinnamon. And like a kid who had gotten into the cookie jar, he sprinkled a thick coating of the sweet reddish spice on his toast, slice after slice. "Don't tell Bar," he giggled. "She'll kill me if she see this."

Bill and Hillary

While the first President Bush had a reputation for being out of touch, Bill Clinton had the ability to make you feel that you were the only person he was talking to, and that whatever was bothering you he not only understood fully, but also that he suffered from the same malady. When Bush said, "I care," people yawned and grumbled, "Yeah, right." But when Clinton bit his lower lip, gave a little grimace and said, "I feel your pain," people wanted to rush to show him where it hurt.

Nowhere was the Clinton empathy on better display than on the campaign trail when he was out to convince people to give him their vote. Like a shy-but-ardent suitor trying to get up enough nerve to ask the best-looking girl in the class to go to the prom, Clinton did everything but get down on one knee to make his pitch. But his ardor always overcame his shyness. There was always time to shake another hand, slap another back and make one more pitch to gain that one extra vote, no matter how far he had to travel or how late the hour.

Clinton launched one of those patented late-hour pitches during the 1996 presidential campaign when he made an unscheduled stop at a Friday night high school football game in South Dakota. It came at the tail end of a week-long September trip that took the presidential entourage to five Western states, including a visit to the Grand Canyon, which made pretty pictures for the TV cameras. So when White House press secretary Mike McCurry said we would add on a sixth state, South Dakota, during the flight back home to Washington from the West Coast, the weary press corps gave a collective groan. The extra stop meant one more story to file and getting home long after midnight instead of the scheduled 8 p.m.

It was drizzling and chilly when Air Force One and the trailing chartered press plane touched down in the dark at the Sioux Falls, S.D. airport. We then loaded onto buses and lined up behind Clinton's shiny, black bulletproof limousine, rain drops on its surface reflecting the flashing red lights of state police cruisers sent to escort this most important visitor.

The presidential motorcade slowly wound its way across some 20 miles of prairie highway that snaked west to the high school. Grousing about the rain and the late hour, reporters glumly peered out the windows of their buses at the pitch-dark countryside. We could see the stadium lights glowing in the distance, looking like a giant space ship that had landed in the middle of a black sea.

As the motorcade approached the stadium, a collective roar went up from the crowd. It was nearly halftime, and Clinton, in jeans, brown cowboy boots and a brown suede jacket, was brought to a tent that had been set up behind the end zone. There, during the half-time intermission, he met with players on the two teams and posed for pictures with them and their cheerleaders. Out on the field, the high school marching band was performing for the crowd a medley of Beatles tunes, ending their program with a spirited, if somewhat dissonant, "Eleanor Rigby," a lament that is hardly the stuff of marching bands and their tubas, cymbals, snare drums and glockenspiels.

Back in the nearly empty tent, a red-eyed Clinton - looking weary after a week of campaigning on the road - heard the music and gave a slight smile. Time to ramp it up for one more campaign pitch. He glanced at Hillary, took a deep breath and exhaled slowly. Upon hearing himself introduced, he bounded up on the makeshift wooden plank stage set up under the goal posts and waved to the screaming throng. Then, without missing a beat, he shouted, "Wow! 'Eleanor Rigby!' That's one of my favorite Beatles songs! Isn't this band great?" The cheers cascaded down from the bleachers in waves and by then everyone had forgotten about the lateness of the hour and the bone-chilling rain, which was still coming down. Bill Clinton was on.

Clinton is the only politician I covered who could set a crowd cheering by extolling the virtues of slaughtering thousands of chickens. All in a good cause, of course - the creation of jobs. But when he got up in front of a crowd and turned on the charm, he could make people applaud for more air pollution. Or as Haley Barbour, now the governor of Mississippi and formerly the Republican National Committee chairman during the early years of the Clinton presidency, used to put it, "Bill Clinton is the Elmer Gantry of politics. He could sell Chevys to Ford dealers."

I got a chance to find out just how good Clinton's personal campaigning skills were long before most Americans knew who he was, let alone that he harbored ambitions to run for president. It was April 1986, and I was sent to Little Rock to write a story about how this progressive young Arkansas governor, a shining symbol of the New South, was being challenged in a Democratic primary by a former Arkansas governor, the aging Orval Faubus, whose name was synonymous with the segregationist past of the Old South.

Faubus, many will recall, was the Arkansas governor who in September 1957 stubbornly defied a Federal Court order to desegregate Little Rock's all-white Central High School. A frustrated President Eisenhower, who had tried to keep the smoldering situation from igniting into a conflagration, was forced to order U.S Army troops from the 101st Airborne Division, the famed Screaming Eagles, to escort nine courageous black teenagers into the school past taunting crowds of white people that lined the sidewalks, shook their fists and shouted curses as the youngsters filed in. In many ways, those stark black-and-white pictures beamed across the nation and around the world probably did more to shock Americans into confronting the reality of racial discrimination than any of the speeches, lectures, demonstrations and court decisions up to that point.

Faubus, by now a tired, washed-up politician at age 76, was storming back out into the political arena for one last sad hurrah. But he was no match for the charismatic Clinton, either in money or political skills. I figured that out quickly.

The first morning I was there, I had a long, windy interview with Faubus. Seated in an empty hotel function room, chairs and tables strewn around like balls scattered on a pool table, he tried to put his own spin on history. He asserted that he had nothing against integration per se, but that he was only trying to preserve states' rights against the power of Washington and protect the safety of the youngsters by ordering National Guard troops to block the school door. He seemed like a nice enough man. Time had erased any outward trace of the old defiance. He said he was running for governor again because Clinton had made a mess of things and he knew how to put things right. But I think he was really running to exorcise some of those old demons that must have haunted him in the nearly 30 years that had passed since he became a much-reviled household name.

After the interview, I caught up with Clinton, who was going out on the road for a day of campaigning in rural Northeast Arkansas. He was riding in a large white Chevy Suburban escorted in front and back by two State Police cruisers. It was agreed that I would join the mini-motorcade by sandwiching my little white, rented Plymouth Horizon between the Clinton van and the police car holding up the rear. So I slipped into place and we were off. But when we got on the Interstate heading north, the Clinton van and the police car in the vanguard took off like a shot, leaving me in the dust. I pressed the accelerator of the little Plymouth all the way to the floor, but the best it would do was sputter and cough its way up to 65 mph. No faster. By now, I was losing sight of the Clinton van and the police cruiser on my tail was right up on my rear bumper. I looked in the mirror and saw the trooper waving his arms and motioning me to go faster. I held up my arms to signal that I was going as fast as I could. He then blew the horn and pulled alongside of me. He again waved his arm, exhorting me to speed up. Somewhat embarrassed and feeling a little like Pa Kettle, I weakly smiled and shook my head back and forth, mouthing that the darn car would not go any faster. He finally got the message, waved, and sprinted off. So my little Plymouth and I motored our merry way up to the town of Piggott where I knew Clinton was headed, hoping that I would be able to find the diner where he was scheduled to speak.

Just as I entered the dusty town, I noticed a diner on the right that had a parking lot full of cars. Then I saw the police cruisers and the Clinton van so I knew this must be the place. I went in and found Clinton working the crowd, shaking hands, slapping backs, laughing, joking and having a grand old time. Waitresses in pink-and-white uniforms and hair nets scurried around filling coffee mugs and serving donuts. The townspeople that packed the booths and stood in the aisles, many in overalls, plaid shirts and mesh-topped trucker hats, seemed to be enjoying the chance to see their young governor up close and in their own backyard.

Someone stuck a chair in the middle of the long, narrow eatery and Clinton climbed up on it, drawing a cheer before he even said a word. Pulling himself to his full 6-2 height, and adjusting his voice so that it had just the right amount of Arkansas twang to be familiar to the folks of this region, he thanked them for coming, told a couple of jokes about pigs and cows and launched into a report on all the good things he was doing to make their lives and the lives of their fellow Arkansans better. He talked about improving education quality and raising teacher pay. He talked about building roads and bridges and he talked about creating jobs. It was here that he drew the cheers for the killing of chickens. It seems that Clinton had negotiated a deal with Tyson Foods, an Arkansas-based chicken producer, to build a new processing plant in the job-starved region he was visiting. So when he told the crowd that the plant would "kill 2,000 chickens a day and create 200 new jobs," thunderous cheers erupted. Encouraged by the enthusiastic response he got, Clinton incorporated the line into every one of the three other speeches he made that day, drawing lusty hoorahs every time. Never was the killing of chickens cheered so loudly. And never had I seen such a natural campaigner who seemed equally at ease at the podium of a Chamber of Commerce breakfast in Little Rock as at the counter of a diner in Piggott.

We wound up the day in Jonesboro, home of Arkansas State University, where Clinton was going to stay at the local Holiday Inn. Walking into the hotel with the governor, I remarked that after a long, day on the hot dusty road, all I wanted was an ice-cold beer. Clinton broke into a laugh. I wondered what was so funny. "Jonesboro is dry," one of the trooper bodyguards said. Oh, no. Clinton looked amused. We walked into the restaurant, sat down and had some ice tea and relived the experiences of the day. Clinton was gracious and took the time to find out a little more about me and what kind of story I was planning to write.

Later, when I had retired to my room, I heard a knock on the door. It was one of the troopers. He handed me a six-pack of cold beer. I don't know where he got it. But the next morning, rested and ready for another day of rural campaigning, Clinton asked me if I enjoyed the beer. I told him I did and thanked him. "Don't thank me," he said, feigning that he didn't know where the beer had come from. What I didn't tell him was that I wrote down in my notebook, "This guy has a national future. He's too good to stay locked in Arkansas."

While Bill Clinton remains the ultimate campaigner, his wife, Hillary Rodham Clinton, showed herself to be quite skilled at the art herself when she was warming up for her run for the Senate in New York in 2000. That considerable skill was on full display in May 1999 when she as first lady went on a Southwest tour to champion a set of historic sites in New Mexico and Colorado that needed federal funds for preservation, a cause she was directly involved in. I was one of only two reporters who went along on the trip, so I got a rare chance to see her up close and make a first-hand assessment of how she might fare in the wilds of New York should she decide to seek the seat being vacated by the retiring Sen. Daniel Patrick Moynihan. After watching and listening for three days, I concluded that she would do just fine.

The trip began in Littleton, Colo., where the Clintons had met privately with the families of the victims of the Columbine High School shootings, which occurred a month earlier, leaving 14 students and one teacher dead. It was the Clintons' first visit to Columbine since the shootings and they were appropriately somber when they hand-in-hand walked out of the Catholic church where the meetings were held and stepped into the waiting presidential limousine. From there they motorcaded over to Dakota Ridge High School. The Clintons entered a raucous gymnasium that was decked out more for a pep rally rather than a memorial gathering, as billed. The Columbine High marching band was blaring out fight songs and costumed cheerleaders were exhorting the crowd to join in a cheer that shouted out the letters of the school. Everywhere there were signs and tee-shirts that read, "We are Columbine," as if to say, "We are famous and you are not!" I know that the shirts and signs and cheers and chants are seen by some as a good way to help overcome the pain and shock of the rampage. But to me, it seemed that the atmosphere was just a little too festive for an event that followed so closely on the heels of the tragedy, After all, only one month had passed since the shootings. The Clintons were introduced to the strains of "Hail to the Chief." The cheering audience spontaneously broke into chants of "We are Columbine!" Caught up in the moment, Clinton, when he rose to speak, asked for the cheer to be repeated, and led the applause and cheers from the podium. From that moment of merriment, the president quickly shifted gears. Quoting from Scripture, he launched into a somber speech about the tragedy and the courage of those who were carrying on. "It's been a long hard month for all of you and a long hard month for America," he said.

After the event, the first lady began her historic preservation tour, which took her to New Mexico and Colorado. One stop was at the remote Acoma Indian Pueblo on the New Mexico desert about 90 miles west of Albuquerque. There, high on a windswept sandstone mesa she visited a former Catholic church, still maintained by the Indians, that dated back to the Spanish occupation of the 15th Century. It featured magnificent hand-painted wooden frescoes that were in the midst of a restoration and preservation project. Clinton came bearing federal funds to aid the project. After visiting the church, Mrs. Clinton - dressed in khaki pants, brown suede hiking boots and a tan suede jacket - toured the primitive village on the mesa, which still had no running water. In honor of the visit, Acoma families, some in native costume, stood silently in front of their tiny adobe-walled, tin-roofed houses as the first lady strolled their dusty, narrow streets. Some of the men were veterans and proudly wore their American Legion hats and medals on their shirts. The residents presented her with gifts of their native pottery and clothing as she passed. Some shyly asked her to pose for pictures, which she did. She even autographed the back of one little girl's tee-shirt with a pink marking pen. As she went, she examined their art work and asked questions about their technique in etching the fine clay pottery for which the Acoma are famous.

"Mrs. Clinton, may I please give you a hug?" pleaded Olivia Sanchez, 65, as Clinton passed her house.

The two women embraced and chatted for a few moments.

After the first lady passed, Sanchez shook her head in amazement. "She's such a strong person. She's gone down and come up every time. I hope she will leave some of her strength with us. Our people need strength," she said.

After touring the pueblo, Mrs. Clinton motored down to the Sky City Community School, a Bureau of Indian Affairs school on the Acoma reservation. About 100 students and teachers were sitting on the floor of the gymnasium as the first lady entered the room. They quickly stood and applauded politely, and sat back down on the floor when she spoke at a microphone set up near the front of the high-ceilinged room. About 15 feet in front of Clinton, an older woman was kneeling as if in prayer, hands clasped in front of her chest as she looked with awe upon the first lady. Tears were running down her face. After her talk, Hillary waded into the crowd and greeted the youngsters and their teachers.

"Hillary! Hillary! Shake my hand!" children excitedly shouted as she carefully stepped her way through the seated audience. Few were disappointed. She shook most of them.

When she reached the kneeling women who had been crying when she spoke, the woman grabbed her arm and pulled her face close to hers.

"I know you have trouble in your family," the woman whispered into Mrs. Clinton's ear. It was an obvious reference to the Monica Lewinsky affair that had been dominating the headlines for more than a year. "I wish the best for you and your husband. I feel so sad. Whatever has happened in the past, just continue to be happy. May you both be blessed." Mrs. Clinton, with tears in her eyes, embraced the woman and kissed her. "Thank you and bless you," she said.

Afterward, I asked the woman who she was and why she was crying when the first lady spoke. She said she was Ida Madalena, 63, a teacher's aide at the school. She said the tears were tears of joy.

"She is such an important person," Madalena said. "Nobody that important has ever visited our reservation. We are so honored."

When it came to taking vacations, the Clintons chose chic settings and enjoyed attending parties and schmoozing with celebrities. While in the White House, they had no summer home of their own. They didn't have a winter home, either. So when they wanted to take a vacation, someone would arrange to have them stay at the private estate or villa of some wealthy supporter - whether it be Hilton Head, S.C. for Renaissance Weekend, the U.S. Virgin Islands just after the New Year, Martha's Vineyard or Jackson Hole, Wyo. in summer or Coronado Beach near San Diego in the spring. But unlike the elder Bush, who mostly stayed put once he arrived at his house, Clinton liked to keep on the move. On vacation, he quickly grew bored with reading mystery novels or playing cards or Scrabble with daughter Chelsea. So while in Martha's Vineyard, where he vacationed for five summers during his presidency, when boredom got the best of him he would go on a shopping expedition into Edgartown or more often, to the golf course where he would engage in marathon rounds of golf, sometimes playing well into the Vineyard's mosquito-laden dusk. Reporters assigned to cover him would grouse at the lateness of the hour as they rubbed themselves down with greasy insect repellant waiting for the president to finish his round. In the evening, he and wife Hillary whirled and twirled into the night from party to party, hosted by celebrities such as *Washington Post* publishing mogul Katharine Graham, former first lady Jacqueline Kennedy Onassis, Washington power lawyer Vernon Jordan and pop singer Carly Simon. The Clintons also were treated to an annual luncheon cruise aboard a 70-foot yacht captained by Massachusetts Sen. Edward Kennedy and packed with Kennedy family members. "Clintons in Camelot" read a headline in USA TODAY over a picture of the celebrity summer boat party. Everyone was wearing sunglasses.

In 1995 and 1996, when he was planning his re-election campaign, Clinton skipped his usual Martha's Vineyard idyll and chose to vacation in Jackson Hole, Wyoming, high in the breathtakingly scenic Grand Teton range of the Rocky Mountains. The site selection, we later found out, was influenced by a poll that asked independent swing voters, who could be pivotal in the election, whether the first family should take a mountain or seaside vacation. The mountains won. Former Clinton adviser Dick Morris, in his memoir "Behind the Oval Office," wrote that he told Clinton "it was politically unwise to project himself as a populist while vacationing on an island with the rich and famous."

So the Clintons, bowing to swing-voter preferences, spent two weeks in August 1995 in Jackson Hole, but hardly in populist style. They stayed at the Bar B Bar Ranch, an 800-acre spread owned by financier Max Chapman. The posh property offered horseback riding, a full gym, a rock-climbing wall, wilderness trails and an observatory, which fascinated Chelsea. While there, the Clintons were photographed in outings of white-water rafting, mountain hiking, camping and horseback riding along rocky trails. Of course, there were still the golf and the parties, which Clinton managed to find in the homes of well-heeled residents of the rich resort who were only too eager to host the president and his wife. One included actor Harrison Ford. Hillary Clinton took time out from all the recreation to attend a party at Jackson Lake Lodge marking the 75th anniversary of women's suffrage. The president was reported to have played over 200 holes of golf during his 17-day stay.

The Clintons also vacationed in Jackson Hole for a week in July 1996 while the Republicans were holding their National Convention in San Diego, nominating Bob Dole to run against the president in the November election. That vacation was more low key, with Clinton trying to project a businesslike image as the election approached. While there, he did two public events, one announcing an end to a gold mining project in Yellowstone National Park and another signing legislation favorable to the oil and gas industry. In their final four years in the White House, with no more re-election campaigns to worry about, the Clintons never took another vacation in Jackson Hole. They returned to Martha's Vineyard three times, instead.

But in 1999, they introduced a new wrinkle to their summer holiday. With Hillary Clinton planning a run for the U.S. Senate seat from New

York being vacated by the retiring Sen. Daniel Patrick Moynihan, the Clintons tacked five days in New York State to the end of their Martha's Vineyard respite. First they went to the Hamptons, the trendy summer playground of Manhattan's chi-chi set on the eastern edge of Long Island. There they were hosted by movie producer Stephen Spielberg, attended a fundraiser in the home of fashion designer Vera Wang and rocked at another fundraiser in an airplane hangar filled with very preppy-looking young people. Hip-hop artist Wycliff Jean headlined the show.

The next day, they flew upstate to Skaneateles, N.Y., a trim and pretty Finger Lakes community about 20 miles southwest of Syracuse where they wowed Upstate New Yorkers hungry for a chance to rub elbows with celebrities. The town was decked out in red-white-and-blue bunting in honor of the presidential visit. And again, rather than stay put at the lakeside mansion owned by millionaire real estate developer Thomas McDonald, the Clintons were out and about daily. Wherever they traveled in the mostly Republican region of Central New York, polite, enthusiastic and almost-adoring crowds greeted them, including 2,500 at Syracuse's Hancock International Airport when Air Force One touched down. Local newspapers, radio and TV stations were saturated with reports of the visit, down to details of what they ate for dinner and how many cars were in their motorcade. Everywhere, the talk was of the first family. Rumors of their movements were the buzz of the town.

Strategically picking their sites to appeal to a broad array of voters should Hillary decide to run for the Senate - we all know now that she did, successfully - they visited former secretary of State William Seward's meticulously preserved mansion in Auburn, N.Y. He served during the Civil War years in the Lincoln administration and was one of the Great Emancipator's closest confidantes. Once a political rival of Lincoln for the presidency, as secretary of state he engineered the purchase of Alaska from Russia, which at that time was laughed at far and wide as "Seward's Folly."

From there, the First Family went to the nearby farmstead of African-American heroine Harriet Tubman, the runaway slave who helped other slaves escape to freedom via the Underground Railroad. In the late 1800s, Tubman bought the farm cheap from Seward.

The Clintons also motorcaded from Skaneateles to the Women's Rights Historical Park at Seneca Falls, N.Y., site of the 1848 convention that kicked off the drive for women's suffrage. There, they signed autographs and studied the displays. As the first couple was preparing to leave, one of the rangers complimented the president on his knowledge of the women's rights movement and jokingly suggested he come back to give tours. "I can work cheap," Clinton replied with a chuckle. "I've got a good pension." We all know now that Clinton doesn't work that cheap now that he is no longer president. He got a $10 million advance for his best-selling autobiography, "My Life." And on the speaking circuit he commands upwards of $100,000 per speech. One can only guess what he would charge to conduct tours at the Women's Rights Historical Park.

Earlier in that political week in the late summer of 1999, the First Family engaged in a time-honored New York political rite by making their first visit to the State Fair in Syracuse. Hillary Clinton, with the president and daughter Chelsea in tow, received an enthusiastic greeting from fairgoers who waited hours to catch a glimpse of her. "So nice to see you. Thank you for coming," she said over and over as she worked her way for more than 90 minutes through a sea of outstretched hands eager to shake hers. Dairy producers and senior citizens were being honored at the fair the day the Clintons visited. So the first lady sampled New York-produced milk and ice cream and shook the hands of a lot of older folks as she made her way around the dairy hall and the quilting exhibits. As the president also worked the crowd with Chelsea, it was hard to tell which of the Clintons was the bigger attraction. At one point, the master presidential campaigner stepped back to watch his wife perform. "I think she's doing just fine without my help," he declared with a satisfied smile.

President Clinton also used part of that 1999 vacation to help the Democratic National Committee and its subsidiary units collect nearly $2 million for the 2000 election campaigns by headlining four fund-raising parties on Long Island. Hillary further used the trip to begin filling her own Senate Exploratory Committee strongbox by collecting at least $550,000 in four fund-raising events, two in Massachusetts and two in New York. With $400,000 from the DNC haul earmarked for her committee as well, she went home from her vacation with nearly $1 million in the bank.

But unlike the two Bushes, Clinton seldom had his vacation interrupted by major crises overseas. Domestic crises were another matter. Who can forget the images of the Clintons' strained departure from the

White House for vacation at Martha's Vineyard on Aug. 18, 1998, shortly after the president admitted his sexual dalliance with former White House intern Monica Lewinsky? There they were walking across the South Lawn to the waiting helicopter - Chelsea, 18, in the middle holding both her parents' hands, the president to her right firmly gripping the leash of the family's brown Labrador Retriever Buddy, the first lady to her left, somber and silent, staring straight ahead through big dark sunglasses. The couple did not speak to each other on the way out to the helicopter or later when they stepped off the plane at the airport on Martha's Vineyard. They separately greeted well-wishers on the tarmac and whisked off into seclusion at the 20-acre Oyster Pound oceanfront compound donated by Boston real estate developer Richard. L. Friedman. But two days later, Clinton dashed off to Washington to tell the nation that he had ordered air and missile strikes on Afghanistan and Sudan in retaliation for the terrorist bombings two weeks earlier at U.S. embassies in Kenya and Tanzania. Critics immediately charged that Clinton ordered the strikes to draw attention away from his personal problems. Whatever the purpose of the strikes, they did indeed take some of the media attention away from the first family's crisis, at least for a few days. Meanwhile, Clinton returned to Martha's Vineyard to continue his vacation.

"W"

The most tumultuous presidential administration I covered is that of George W. Bush, the 43rd president of the United States. An economic recession, the September 11 terrorist attacks, the wars in Afghanistan and Iraq, corporate scandals, high gas prices and Hurricane Katrina, perhaps the worst natural disaster to strike the country, all burst onto the scene before he had completed five years on the job. No president since Franklin Roosevelt has had to deal with such a broad array of issues and problems. This is not to say other presidents didn't have it tough. All presidents have it tough. No job is tougher. Bush was widely praised for his bold and decisive leadership in the aftermath of the September 11 attacks. He also was widely praised when the war in Iraq looked like a slam dunk. But he was forced onto the defensive as insurgent attacks in Iraq escalated and the American death toll mounted. Then Hurricane Katrina hit Louisiana, Mississippi and Alabama, causing billions of dollars in damage, killing more than 1,200 people and forcing the evacuation of a flooded New Orleans. Bush was roundly criticized for what at first blush appeared to be a slow and inadequate federal response. His poll ratings took a nosedive and public confidence in his leadership dwindled. Covering that White House day to day is like going to work in a snowstorm that never seems to let up. As soon as you shovel out the driveway, it is full again. Then, you have to start over. It is always something.

One of my first encounters with George W. Bush came in 1989, 11 years before he became president, while he was visiting his father, then the president, at the family's summer home in Kennebunkport, Me. There, he showed a playful sense of humor, especially when it came to egging his father on. One May Saturday morning at Walker's Point, after the elder Bush and wife Barbara finished taping a boat safety commercial, George W. dared his father to dive into the chilly coastal water. The president asked how much he would give him to do it. George W. reached into his pockets and came up with $11.

"Put the money down," the president said.

The son laid it on the dock.

"Don't you dare," Barbara said, her eyes narrowing as she watched her husband pull off his shirt and remove his boat shoes and socks. If he heard her threat, it made no difference. He turned and neatly dove into the black water, khaki pants and all. Several Bush grandchildren gathered on the dock cheered and applauded.

"George!" a horrified Barbara shouted.

Down in the water, a sputtering Bush, looking smug, like a kid who had won a bet, surfaced and paddled around for a few seconds. "It's wonderful," he said. "Got to be 60 (degrees). Good signal for the bluefish coming in."

The dripping president climbed out of the water, picked up his cash and asked how much he could get if he did it again. The kids came up with $1.98 and George W. offered an additional $20. But Barbara would have none of it.

"George. Get into that house and get dry. You are going to catch cold," she scolded.

The elder Bush, his wet hair plastered to his scalp, obediently picked up his shirt, shoes and socks, gave a quick wave and padded off. A picture of that dive, taken by Associated Press photographer Scott Applewhite, still hangs in the White House press room.

But "W," in those early days, also showed a temper. One August morning on the golf course with his father at Kennebunkport, an overzealous woman reporter new on the beat and unfamiliar with the protocol of not asking questions when the presidential party was lining up to swing, repeatedly asked the elder Bush questions about the looming war in the Persian Gulf. "W," standing behind his father, and getting a little hotter under the collar with each question, finally had enough and turned to the offending reporter. "Hey! Can't you see we're trying to shoot here? Can it!" he shouted. The chagrined woman shrunk back. In silence, the Bush foursome teed off and quickly zoomed on.

The contrast between the elder Bush's summer home in coastal Kennebunkport and the younger Bush's 1,600-acre ranch in Crawford, Texas could not have been sharper. Where one was kissed by cooling sea breezes, the other was smothered by oppressive summer heat. Where at one you could sit on the porch and gaze far out to sea, at the other the only sea in view is the rolling prairie dotted by scrub brush and bending trees that seem to be sailing against the wind.

"W" has carefully tried to make his time at his ranch look like working vacations, which they are, to some degree. Rather than go to Crawford for the month of August and stay there, he has used the ranch as his base and traveled out from time-to-time around the country making speeches and raising campaign funds. In August 2002, with the economy in the doldrums, he staged an economic summit in nearby Waco, which featured business leaders, economists and government officials discussing how to make things better. Critics booed it as just a cheap publicity stunt. But a few weeks later, armed with advice he got at the summit, he came out with a proposal for a second round of tax cuts, which were enacted after much partisan squabbling, in 2003.

In between his travel and staged events, Bush basically stays in seclusion on the ranch, clearing brush, mending fences, fishing in his pond and leisurely driving his dusty white Ford F-150 pickup truck around his own four-mile dirt road that winds along dry creek beds, through small valleys, past rocky canyons and across prairie grassland. Beef cattle owned by a neighbor next door graze in the hot summer sun. No posh parties. No extended golf outings. And on occasions when he wants to meet the press and hold a news conference, he often journeys about seven miles down the road to the Coffee Station - a combination coffee shop and gas station on Crawford's main crossroads - and holds forth in the parking lot. No frills there. But on the day after Thanksgiving in 2004, Bush, casually dressed in tan jeans, brown cowboy boots and a green plaid shirt did make note that some of the reporters who came to cover him might have been taking the informality a little too far. He pointed out that several scribes in the entourage "forgot to shave," eliciting a chagrined "Aww" from the stubble-faced offenders.

"Well, I was just curious," Bush said, undaunted. "It looks like it's contagious, as a matter of fact."

Like his father, "W" has used his summer home to hold meetings with visiting foreign leaders - Russian President Vladimir Putin, Chinese President Jiang Zemin, Japanese Prime Minister Junichiro Koizumi, British Prime Minister Tony Blair, Saudi Arabian Prince Abdullah, Italian Prime Minister Silvio Berlusconi and Australian Prime Minister John Howard, among them. However, an invitation to the ranch is something special in the eyes of the president. He only invites foreign leaders he likes. We can draw some conclusions when we note that among those not invited so far are French President Jacques Chirac and German Chancellor Gerhard Schroeder, two vocal opponents of the war in Iraq.

Japan's Koizumi is one leader Bush really likes. You can see it in the ease with which they joke when they are together and in the way the president describes their friendship when he is out making speeches. Bush once presented Koizumi, a big baseball fan, with a fielder's glove given to him by future Hall of Famer Cal Ripken Jr. In 2004, Koizumi threw out the first pitch in Yankee Stadium for a crucial September game between the New York Yankees and Boston Red Sox. And Bush likes to note that Koizumi is a big Elvis Presley fan. Koizumi often sings Elvis songs in public and shares the same January 8 birthday with the rock-and-roll legend. But most of all, Bush cites the U.S.-Japan relationship as a model for how two countries once at war can become friends and work together for peace.

"After World War II, my predecessor, Harry S. Truman, believed that we should work with the Japanese to build a democracy," Bush said in his 2004 acceptance speech at the Republican National Convention. "A lot of people in this country questioned the wisdom. You can understand why. There was a lot of bitterness toward the Japanese.

"But there were folks in this country that believed in the power of liberty to transform an enemy into an ally. And so they did the hard work after World War II, developing that country and to build that country into a democracy. And because of that work, today I talk to Prime Minister Koizumi talking about the peace we all want, talking about how to make the world more peaceful."

That speech then went well beyond letting bygones be bygones:

"When you hear me say I believe in the transformational power of liberty, think about the fact that the American president and the leader of Japan are working together for peace," he said. "Some day — some day — some day an American president and a duly-elected leader of Iraq will sit down at the table to talk about peace, and our children and our grandchildren will be better off for it."

Underscoring the good relations between the U.S. and Japan, just three days after Hurricane Katrina hit on Aug. 29, 2005, the Japanese government said it would supply up to $300,000 in emergency assistance for supplies such as tents, blankets, power generators and portable water tanks from a supply depot maintained by the Japanese in Florida. Shortly after, it gave $200,000 to the Red Cross. Then came another $700,000 in assistance, increasing the total to $1.2 million. In a phone call to Bush, Koizumi pledged that his government would work with all U.S. disaster assistance agencies to help in any way it could.

Of Bush's many ranch hostings, the November 2001 drop-in by Putin was most visibly remarkable. Bush took his Russian guest to Crawford High School where the two leaders engaged in a colloquy with students gathered in a packed gymnasium. To those old enough to remember the Cold War and the days when the Soviet Union was the great enemy, the sight of Bush and Putin side by side, neckties left back at the ranch, laughing and joking easily with the students, was truly amazing. These were the grandchildren that former Soviet leader Nikita Khrushchev once boldly vowed would grow up under communism — kids whose parents as students in the 1950s and 1960s cowered under school desks during drills aimed at protecting them from a rain of Soviet nuclear bombs. Half a century later, the Bush-Putin talks focused on how the U.S. and Russia could reduce nuclear weapon stockpiles and cooperate as allies in the war against terrorism.

As Bush noted at the high school, "A lot of people never really dreamt that an American president and a Russian president could have established the friendship that we have. When I was in high school, Russia was an enemy. Now, the high school students can know Russia as a friend; that we're working together to break the old ties, to establish a new spirit of cooperation and trust so that we can work together to make the world more peaceful."

Added a gracious Putin, "Together, we can achieve quite a lot, especially if we are helped in this by such a young and active and beautiful generation as the one we are meeting with now."

The audience also included exchange students from Russia studying in the United States. The remarks by the two presidents drew enthusiastic applause.

Keeping the mood light, Bush called for questions from the kids and joked that math questions would be out of bounds. One eighth grader asked Putin what he liked about Texas. In his best diplomatic style, he replied, "We in Russia have known for a long time that Texas is the most important state in the United States." He went on to note that like Texas, Russia produces oil and there are many business contracts between Russians and Texans. A senior asked about U.S. plans to build a nuclear defense shield. Another asked if the agreement to reduce nuclear weapons meant the warheads would be destroyed, or only taken out of service. "Destroyed," Bush replied.

Putin's answer was more circuitous. He remarked that the technical knowledge displayed by the questioner caused him to wonder if he were at NASA headquarters in Houston rather than Crawford High. "Looking at the questions of the 12th graders, it comes to my mind that everything is fine with this nation and in this school," Putin said.

A senior girl asked Bush if he had advice for them as they go out into the world. Without missing a beat, Bush replied, "Listen to your mother! Trust the Lord, too." She then asked the Russian president if he liked the barbecue served at the Bush ranch. "I had a hard time imagining how could a living person create such a masterpiece of cooking. A fantastic meal," the Russian president answered with a smile. A seventh grader asked Bush if he would take Crawford students with him if he goes to Russia. Bush said no. But Putin quickly jumped in, asking students to — on the count of three — raise their hands and shout "yes" if they wanted Bush to visit Russia. The ayes had it. The following year, Bush visited Russia.

But for all the public atmospherics, what is said privately in the meetings back at the ranch usually turns out to be more important. News reports out of that session between Bush and Putin said that the two leaders failed to agree on whether the 1972 Anti-Ballistic Missile Treaty between the United States and the Soviet Union should be scrapped, as proposed by Bush, but opposed by Putin. A month later, Bush backed out of the treaty. And Putin surprised the world with his muted criticism. "Russia quiet as Bush plans withdrawal from missile pact," read a headline in USA TODAY. Analysts credited the close personal relationship Bush cultivated with Putin for the easy Russian acquiescence.

While the results of those ranch meetings have not always immediately been apparent, they often have shown up in subtle-but-critical ways down the road. Bush's meeting with Chinese President Jiang Zemin in October 2002 led to an increase in U.S.-China cooperation on critical issues such as getting North Korea to abandon its nuclear weapons program.

And in late August 2002, with war in Iraq looking more and more inevitable, Bush invited to the ranch Prince Bandar bin Sultan, the Saudi Arabian ambassador to the U.S. Those meetings were largely billed as a failure because Bandar came out saying the Saudis still opposed war with Iraq. Maybe so. But the *Washington Post* reported on April 27, 2003 that shortly after the Bush-Bandar meeting, Gen. Richard Myers, chairman of the Joint Chiefs of Staff, flew to Saudi Arabia. The Saudis denied that the visit had anything to do with the looming war in Iraq. But in retrospect, the *Post* article said, "The Myers trip marked the start of five months of intensive military cooperation between Washington and Riyadh that played a crucial role in the U.S. victory over Saddam Hussein. According to sources close to the negotiations, Saudi Arabia ended up agreeing to virtually every request made by the Bush administration for military or logistical assistance." The Bush-Bandar meeting at the ranch might have paved the way for that.

But try as Bush might to rest and relax at his ranch, it just never seemed to be in the cards. Political opponents, taking advantage of a White House press corps stuck in Crawford and hungry for news, staged protest events to gain their attention. From abortion rights marches to demonstrations against the Israeli pullout of Gaza, Crawford became a magnet for those looking to score points at Bush's expense. But none was more effective than Cindy Sheehan, the Vacaville, Calif. mother whose son, Casey, was killed in Iraq in 2004. On Aug. 6, 2005, four days after Bush arrived at this ranch for the summer respite, Sheehan came to Crawford and set up a camp on the side of the road leading to Bush's spread. She came to seek a meeting with the president and urge him to bring all U.S. troops home.

Bush refused to meet with her. He said he sympathized with her loss, but he disagreed with her demand to end the war. Besides, he already met with her in June 2004 at Fort Lewis, Wash., when he visited with several families who had lost loved ones in Iraq. But the vigil of the lone, bereaved mother outside the president's gates was a heart-wrenching scene the news media could hardly resist. And the news coverage at home and abroad triggered a huge outpouring of public sympathy for Sheehan, forcing Bush onto the defensive. It set off a new wave of criticism, not only of the war, but also of Bush's vacationing while Americans were continuing to die in Iraq. Supporters of Sheehan's cause flocked to Crawford to stand in solidarity with her, national and international news media in tow.

Worried that anti-war sentiment was being blown out of proportion by the Sheehan vigil, backers of Bush's Iraq policy organized a counter demonstration in Crawford to show support for U.S. troops. Not to be overshadowed, Sheehan's forces staged a demonstration of their own on the same day. It was quite a scene: Crawford, Texas, population 700, it's main corner an intersection with a blinking light, overrun by as many as 5,000 people who braved 102-degree summer heat to express their Iraq sentiments, pro and con.

A day later, Bush still at the ranch, went before the TV cameras to warn residents of Louisiana, Alabama and Mississippi about the coming Hurricane Katrina. On Monday, he flew to Arizona and California to promote the new Medicare prescription drug benefit for seniors. That was the day the storm hit. It triggered more criticism that Bush was on vacation at a time of crisis.

On Tuesday, as reports of the Katrina's devastation poured in, Bush was in San Diego marking the 60th anniversary of the end of World War II. As critics began to charge that the federal response was inadequate, Bush threw in the towel. His press secretary announced that he would return to Washington, two days before his vacation was scheduled to end.

If there is any lesson here, it is that presidents — all presidents — are never on vacation. And they have to be careful to not look like they are when things are going wrong. Perception is everything.

A few personal things I have learned about Bush: No designer jeans for him. He wears Wranglers. He drinks Texas-brewed Shiner non-alcoholic beer from the bottle. He reads a lot of history books and is much-better read than many of his detractors give him credit for. He is always in a much better mood when he is with his wife, and sometimes on trips seems lost without her. He rarely fails to mention her and sing her praises in his speeches. At times, he gets teary eyed doing it. He can be very gracious and unassuming, like the time he obligingly held our tape recorders in his hand and up to his mouth when my USA TODAY partner Judy Keen and I were worried that the engine noise on Air Force One would muffle his voice during an interview prior to the 2004 GOP Convention. He even held a barbeque at his ranch for reporters in the summer of 2005.

But he also can be sarcastic with reporters. His humor directed at them is sometimes biting. During the 2000 presidential campaign, an open microphone at a Labor Day rally in Naperville, Ill, caught him referring to *New York Times* reporter Adam Clymer as an "asshole." He went all day without talking to reporters after that *faux pas*. But late that evening, upon arriving in Scranton, Pa., he finally agreed to make a statement. Standing in the dark on the Wilkes Barre/Scranton Airport tarmac with only the TV light eerily illuminating his face, Bush said the remark was not for public consumption and that it was not intended to be heard by anyone outside his private circle. Asked if he would apologize to Clymer, Bush repeated his statement that the remark was private. Asked a second time if he would apologize, he unwaveringly repeated his statement once more. Some reporters thought the profanity would cost him points with voters. But others said it only humanized Bush and might have helped him.

The Bush sarcasm was again on display on a 2002 trip to France when he held a joint news conference with French President Jacques Chirac. NBC's David Gregory asked Chirac a question in French. An astounded Bush responded with a zinger. "The guy memorizes four words, and he plays like he's intercontinental," said Bush. As the president began to leave the podium, he shouted to Gregory. "As soon as you get in front of a camera, you start showing off."

On several occasions he has repeated the same biting quip to radio reporters Mark Knoller of CBS and Mark Smith of NBC: "You have a face for radio."

He got back at me after he was displeased with a story I wrote in December 2003. His chance came at a Christmas reception for the media at the White House, about a week after the offending story appeared. I had already been told by press secretary Scott McClellan that Bush had objections to the story. But I saw those objections reflected in his narrowed eyes when my wife Carol and I greeted him. He icily shook my hand and quickly leaned to her and turned on the charm. As we walked away, he shouted out, "At least you married well!"

We Americans ask and expect a lot from our presidents. And then, no matter what they do or how hard they work in our behalf, at least half of us are generally unhappy. And we make our feelings known through a news media only too eager to air our grievances.

Of course, there are times when we rally behind our chief executive. Usually it is in times of war — as long as the war is not too long, doesn't get too messy and not too many Americans get killed. Then, we are back to what has become equilibrium in early 21st century American politics — sharply divided mostly by political party and nasty in the expression of our divisions. Hurricane Katrina appeared to be one of those dramatic events in the course of history where the nation comes together behind its leader. But not this time. Instead of our political leaders standing up, saying we are all in this together and we will do whatever it takes to overcome it, opponents of the president, with the rescue effort still going on, seemed to be angling themselves for political gain by bashing his leadership. So we were back at equilibrium: sharply divided by party, strident in our criticism and unwilling to concede that the presidency is a tough job for any man or woman who takes it on.

Have You Ever Flown On Air Force One?

One of the first questions people ask when they find that I cover the White House is, "Have you ever flown on Air Force One?" The answer is yes, many times over the years. And I have official certificates signed by three presidents attesting to it. In fact, I was on Air Force One flying with President George W. Bush from Waco, Texas to Glendale, Ariz. on the morning of Aug. 29, 2005, when Hurricane Katrina was slamming into Louisiana, Alabama and Mississippi, a tragedy that shook the Bush presidency to its core. We were watching live coverage of the storm as it blasted New Orleans on the Fox News Channel. Air Force One, with its state-of-the-art communications system, can pick up live television broadcasts anywhere it flies. Cell phones work on board, too, although Air Force personnel who manage the president's flying office frown on it.

Back in the press cabin, in the tail of the jumbo custom-designed Boeing 747 jet, there are two plasma TV screens on the forward bulkheads which are used on most flights to show videos of popular movies to the pool of 14 reporters, photographers and camera crew members seated in that section. The press cabin is one of several compartments in the back end of the gleaming blue-and-white presidential jet. They all resemble first-class sections on commercial airliners. Also seated back there is the Air Force crew assigned to the plane, the Secret Service protective detail and other support personnel. In the extreme far end of the tail is the galley from which meals are served.

Although the popular illusion is that the meals served aboard Air Force One are top-of-the-line. They are not. Don't forget. It is an Air Force plane and it serves Air Force food. Breakfast is often a fruit cup, those little frozen pancakes or waffles and either pork sausages or a thin slice of ham. Although, I have to admit that on rare occasion they will surprise us. One breakfast featured the biggest, thickest slice of ham I ever saw. Another was topped by a giant cinnamon bun dripping with creamy, white frosting, bigger even than those monstrous treats you can buy in a mall. A typical lunch is a turkey club or meatball sandwich with potato chips, a chocolate chip cookie and lemonade, served in an oval wicker basket lined with a napkin. Dinners can be lasagna, tenderloin tips or chicken and vegetables, all of which seem to have after come out of a box in the grocer's freezer. Beer and wine are available, but you have to ask for them. No one asks at breakfast or lunch because we are usually on our way to work. But at dinner, when we are heading back to Washington after a full day of events, some reporters like to have a drink with their meal. If you ask for one, the request is honored, but almost with indignation by the military flight attendants doing the serving. They make you feel like you are stepping out of bounds. Those brave enough to ask for that first drink rarely have the nerve to find out what would happen if they went overboard and asked for a second. They would probably be put out at 30,000 feet.

Who pays for all this Air Force One shuttling of reporters? We do. No, not the American taxpayer. The news media. Each news reporter who travels on Air Force One is billed by the government the commercial rate between the cities traveled. That means that if you fly on Air Force One between Washington and St. Louis, your news organization, in my case, USA TODAY, is charged what it would cost to fly on a commercial airliner on that route, and not at any discount rates. Flying aboard Air Force One is not cheap.

The next question people often ask after finding out that I have flown on Air Force One is, "Do all the reporters who travel with Bush ride on Air Force One?" That answer is no, not all at once. Only a rotating media pool of 13 or 14 composed of reporters from the *Associated Press, Reuters, Bloomberg News,* one daily newspaper, one weekly news magazine, one TV network and one radio network, along with three still photographers, and two TV network camera and sound technicians. That way, everyone is covered in case the president, a member of his staff or his press secretary speak or give briefings on board. Then it becomes the responsibility of the pool reporter to share the information with the other reporters on the trip, who travel in a separate chartered commercial airplane. That too is paid for by the news media. The cost of chartering the airliner - arrangements are made by the White House - is shared equally among the news organizations that are traveling. Also not cheap. A typical day trip with the president when he goes to some city in the morning and returns to Washington in the late afternoon can cost $2,500-$3,000 for each reporter traveling. If the trip is an overnighter, the media pay for their hotels and meals, too. But again, the White House makes all necessary arrangements and reservations. Even the charter buses that take us from airport to event or event to hotel. While we pay for all that, having someone else take care of the logistics is a great convenience. All we have to do is show up, and of course, pay the bills. The White House handles the rest.

Information gathered by the pool reporters traveling on Air Force One is shared through what we call a "pool report," written by the print reporter in the pool, i.e., the reporter who works for a daily newspaper. That means me when I am on board. The report is then used by the other reporters as if they were there. The TV and radio pool reporters share their audio and visual tapes. For example, if NBC was the pool reporter, the tape they shoot could air on NBC, CBS, CNN, FOX and any other news outlet that wants it. Here is an excerpt from the print pool report I wrote the morning Katrina struck:

> Pool Report #1
> August 29, 2005
> Waco, Texas to Glendale, Ariz.
> "Marine One touched down, under overcast skies, on the Texas State Technical College tarmac at 9:30 a.m. CDT. The president and Mrs. Bush emerged, strolled straight to Air Force One and boarded quickly. He is wearing a brown suit (highly unusual) white shirt and gold tie. She is wearing a gray pantsuit with a light-blue blouse, collar outside the jacket.
> "We were airborne nine minutes later at 9:39 a.m. CDT.
> "Also on board: Karl Rove and Deputy Chief of Staff Joe Hagin. Scott McClellan is back from vacation. Rather than watch a movie, the press pool elected to keep Fox News coverage of Hurricane Katrina on the TV screens.…..After breakfast, Scott McClellan came back to gaggle. He brought along with him his brother Mark, who directs the Medicare and Medicaid programs at HHS. The elder McClellan briefed on the new prescription drug benefit the president will talk about today.
> "But first, Scott McClellan said the president has been getting regular updates on Hurricane Katrina and helping to make sure the proper federal assistance is provided to the stricken areas. Bush talked earlier this morning, before departing, with FEMA Director Mike Brown. He also talked with him during the flight. Hagin participated in a video

conference aboard Air Force One with state and federal officials directing the hurricane response. He then was to give the president an update. Scott McClellan said the 'top priority' was to make sure the focus of the efforts was on saving lives. Bush also this morning declared Louisiana and Mississippi 'major disaster areas,' which opens the gate for federal financial assistance to homeowners and businesses trying to recover from the storm.

"With regard to reports that the president is considering tapping the Strategic Petroleum Reserve as a way of making up for the loss of refineries shut down by the storm, Scott said the Department of Energy is studying it, but still has not gathered enough information abut the situation on the ground to make a recommendation to Bush. But he did answer 'yes' in response to a question asking if tapping the reserve is an option, noting that 'the reserve is there for emergency situations' such as the natural disaster now being faced. He just said it is 'too early' for a decision yet.......

"Scott McClellan then talked a bit about Tuesday's speech at the Coronado Naval Air Station commemorating the 60th anniversary of the end of World War II. He said that while the speech's primary focus will be honoring those who served in World War II, it also will draw parallels between that war, which saw nations come together to battle a 'murderous ideology,' and the global war on terrorism, which also is a fight against a 'murderous ideology.' The audience will primarily be military personnel and families.

"Later, Bush will visit privately with medical personnel at the base and then with troops wounded in Iraq being cared for at the base hospital.

"Air Force One touched down at Luke Air Force Base at 10:35 a.m. MDT, after a nearly two-hour flight. Greeters included Sen. John Kyl and Sen. John McCain. Kyl, up for re-election next year, went up the gangplank and posed for pictures with the president and the first lady. McCain did not. He stayed down on the tarmac in the bright sun and stood by a table holding a birthday cake placed there in his honor. Today is McCain's 69th birthday. The president and first lady came down and offered their congratulations and posed for more pictures.

"The motorcade, including Kyl, but without McCain, rolled at 10:45 a.m., passing small clusters of supporters along the highway. Among the signs: 'Support Our Troops,' 'Welcome Mr. President,' 'Social Security Reform is Good,' and 'Stay the Course.' As the president's entourage turned into the Pueblo El Mirage RV Resort and Country Club, about 50 shouting protesters stood at the entrance with signs such as 'Bush is a lying (sic) turd,' 'What Noble Cause?' 'War is a Lie' and 'Georgie Girl.' Don't ask for an explanation of that last one.

"Motorcade arrived at 10:56 a.m. MDT. Bush was speaking about 10 minutes later.

"Richard Benedetto
USA TODAY"

Life aboard Air Force One is reflected in the personality and habits of the president. George W. Bush rarely wanders back from his suite at the front of the plane - bedroom/sitting room, full bath, wood-paneled office and conference room - to talk to the reporters on board. But we know that he, like most presidents, holds staff meetings on board and gets regular updates via phone, video conference or coded diplomatic dispatches from aides on the ground and far afield. On the final day of the 2004 campaign, Judy Keen my USA TODAY partner on the White House beat, and one of the best reporters around, wrote that Bush relaxed between stops by playing gin rummy on the plane with his staffers. Also on board that day was Boston Red Sox pitcher Curt Schilling, a Bush fan who then was fresh off his team's heroic first victory in the World Series since 1918.

Bill Clinton was much more of an Air Force One schmoozer. He often came back to chat in the press section, both on and off the record. Clinton sometimes also would on late-night flights back to Washington invite reporters up front to play cards with him, usually Hearts, on condition that everything said during the game was off the record. I never knew how to play Hearts and never sat in.

George H.W. Bush once invited pool reporters up to his office to watch the first game of the 1990 World Series on live TV between the Cincinnati Reds and the Oakland As. The Reds won that series in a 4-0 sweep.

The elder Bush, who was the first president to use the current 747 version of Air Force One, like Clinton, often strolled back to the press section, stemmed glass of white wine in hand, to chat with reporters at the end of a long day on the road. Since he rarely stipulated that the chats were off the record, it meant pool reports would be necessary, hardly a task the weary reporters were eager to perform after an exhausting day. One night, Bush press secretary Marlin Fitzwater came back and said the president was coming aft to chat. The press pool let out a collective groan. Unbeknownst to us, the president was right behind Fitzwater and heard our tired protest. Without missing a beat, he stepped through the door, smiled wryly, held up his glass of wine in toast, said, "Good night, all!" spun on his heel and walked back. That must have been the first and last time reporters turned down a chance to interview the president. We were embarrassed.

President Gerald Ford was occasionally photographed and filmed falling on the stairs of Air Force One or bumping his head on the doorway as he embarked from the aircraft. Those gaffes became the focus for some hilarious skits in the mid-1970s on NBC's *Saturday Night Live,* with a bumbling Ford played in a suit and football helmet by comedian Chevy Chase. Always one to take the joke graciously, Ford even allowed his press secretary, Ron Nessen, to go on the program and play himself in a skit poking fun at his boss.

I never covered Ford when he was president, but I did get a chance to interview him in November 1996 in Grand Rapids, Mich. when he hosted the Republican Governors Association at a reception in the Gerald R, Ford Museum there. The museum, in the town where he grew up, chronicles the former president, vice president and congressman's more than 32 years in public life. At the time, Ford was 83, but looked 20 years younger. When the reception broke up, I fell into step with the 38th president and began interviewing him as he started walking out. Getting interviews from politicians can be like that, especially the bigger ones. You've got to grab them while you can or the opportunity may never arise again. A Secret Service agent began to push me away, but Ford waved him off and went on answering my questions as we continued walking. We came to a large white marble staircase and began stepping down. I was looking at him and trying to write at the same time. I suddenly stumbled and lost my footing. Ford quickly grabbed my arm and prevented me from taking what could have been a nasty tumble down some pretty formidable stone steps. It was quite a turnaround: the so-called clumsy Ford gracefully preventing the hotshot reporter from falling. I thanked him profusely and never uttered a Ford stumbling joke again. They used to joke that Ford couldn't walk and chew gum at the same time. Reporters can't take notes and walk down stairs at the same time.

In addition to Air Force One and the press charter plane that tags along, the traveling presidential road show includes an Air Force cargo plane that flies out ahead of the president carrying his limousines, Secret Service communications vehicles and even his helicopter, if needed. When Air Force One lands, the motorcade is in place and waiting. If the day includes stops in more than one city, two cargo planes are dispatched with duplicate equipment, one to each location. At the same time, uniformed Secret Service personnel have to go out in advance and provide security screening of those who attend the presidential events. The same for Secret Service protective personnel, who go in days in advance to coordinate with local police, map and secure motorcade routes and provide security sweeps of the facilities where the president will be speaking or staying, if the trip is an overnighter.

To be sure, a presidential trip is much more than just a quick flight in and out of town.

A few more Air Force One facts:

There are two identically marked and equipped 747s in the presidential fleet. One is a backup. They are housed in a specially constructed giant hangar at Andrews Air Force Base in suburban Maryland, just outside of Washington, D.C.

Any airplane the president flies in - whether it be the gleaming 747 jumbo jet boldly emblazoned with the words "United States of America" we are all most familiar with, or the similarly marked 757 airliner or sleek Gulfstream jet available for flights into airports unable to accommodate larger planes - is designated "Air Force One" as its identification to ground controllers or other aircraft in the area.

Air traffic in and out of commercial airports is usually stopped when Air Force One is taking off or landing. When possible, presidents fly into military airports to avoid disturbing the usual passenger traffic.

The military green-and-white helicopter that ferries the president is "Marine One" because it is piloted, secured and maintained by the U.S. Marine Corps. When the president helicopters, the press pool accompanies in another Marine helicopter with bench seats along the walls, similar to the ones that carry a Leatherneck rifle platoon into combat. The back end has a motor-driven ramp for entering and exiting.

According to my friend and colleague Ken Walsh, who has written a book on the history of Air Force One, overall, 12 presidents, starting with

Franklin Roosevelt, have flown while in office. John F. Kennedy had the presidential jet painted the way it looks today. Walsh notes that Air Force One has an elaborate security system, much of it classified. However, he says that there are "countermeasure" systems designed to divert incoming missiles if Air Force One came under attack. The sheet aluminum skin of the aircraft is designed to ward off electromagnetic pulses in case of a nuclear strike and allow the plane to retain its communications abilities. When not in use, the plane is protected from would-be saboteurs around the clock by armed military guards. Moreover, if you think security is tight when you go to board a commercial airliner, it is far more strict if you are trying to board Air Force One. All reporters' bags and equipment are sniffed by dogs and thoroughly searched by Secret Service personnel before boarding. And if your name is not on the pre-prepared manifest, forget about talking your way on, Walsh says.

Aircraft that vice presidents travel on are known as "Air Force Two." Vice presidential helicopters are designated "Marine Two." The current most commonly used Air Force Two is a Boeing 757 jetliner with similar markings as Air Force One, but considerably more modest in its furnishings and décor.

In January 1997, when traveling with Vice President Al Gore on Air Force Two, the plane broke down late at night in Boise, Idaho. We had just spent the day visiting floods in Washington state, California and Idaho and were eager to get home to Washington, D. C. We were told we would have to wait four hours to have a new part flown in. Some photographers and TV cameramen on board decided to pass the waiting time by playing poker. Gore, in tee-shirt and jeans, wearily walked around the plane chatting with reporters and talking about the floods and damage we had seen. The photographers invited him to join their card game. You could tell that he wanted to, but always worrying about his image, hesitated, thinking about how it might look if it was reported that the vice president played cards aboard Air Force Two. I, for one, urged him to play, as did others on board. He grimly looked at me, one of only two print reporters on the plane, and said, "I'll play if you don't report it." With a wave of the hand, I pledged that I wouldn't. Gore played, and judging from the laughter emanating from the gathering, seemed to be having a great time. I never reported it - until now. But I often thought over the years that had I written about it at the time, it would have helped humanize Gore and loosen his stiff, robotic image, often the butt of jokes by the late-night TV comics. He has never been able to shake it.

Gore could laugh and joke and have fun. But he seldom did it publicly, Even when he did, it looked strained or staged. Remember him kissing his wife on stage at the 2000 Democratic National Convention?

However, I never saw Gore laugh so hard than when I went to his office in the Old Executive Office building next to the White House in 1998 for an interview. It was scheduled for 6 p.m., which meant that I had to drive there in rush-hour traffic from my office, which was then in Arlington, Va., just across the Potomac River from the capital. I planned on taking a taxi, but it was raining, making it near impossible to get a cab. So I drove over and pulled into a parking garage on Pennsylvania Avenue, one block from the White House. The attendant said the garage was closing at 7 p.m. and I would have to be out by then. I said I could not make it. He suggested an alternative. A garage about four doors down the block on the same side of the street was open until 10 p.m.

Putting my car into reverse, I started backing out, trying to ease my way into Pennsylvania Avenue again. But with the rain and the rush hour, the traffic was bumper-to-bumper. Rather than try to inch my way in and hope that a good Samaritan would make way for me, I decided to skip the street and drive down the sidewalk to the next garage. The downtown sidewalk was plenty wide enough.

So I turned left and drove slowly toward the next garage. Flabbergasted pedestrians thought they were seeing things. A man exiting his office building through a revolving door stopped dead at the sight of a car passing on the sidewalk in front of him. When I pulled into the next garage, the wide-eyed attendant asked incredulously where I came from. "The sidewalk," I blithely answered, handing him the keys and hightailing it out of there.

I arrived at Gore's office, breathless, about 10 minutes late. Upon entering his inner chamber, I apologized profusely and tried to break the ice by relating the story of my drive down the Pennsylvania Avenue sidewalk. Gore began laughing uproariously and laughed and laughed and laughed unlike I or anyone in the general public ever saw him laugh before. It was so infectious that I began laughing, as did others in the room.

When the laughter subsided, I joked that I was stopped by a police officer, but he let me go when I told him I was on the way to a meeting with the vice president. That produced a new round of red-faced laughter from Gore. But then, catching himself, he abruptly stopped and returned to sobriety. "You really didn't tell the officer that, did you?" he asked seriously. "No," I assured him. He apparently felt better that his name not be associated with such a shameful escapade.

Gore will always hold a warm spot in my heart. That is because when he was running for president in 1988, reporters who traveled to his hometown of Carthage, Tenn. to cover his formal announcement of candidacy found a complimentary bottle of Tennessee's own Jack Daniels bourbon in their hotel rooms. It was a first for me, although more-senior reporters observed that free booze from politicians was once a common treat. If so, then that must have been the end of an era. It never happened again.

My longest stint aboard Air Force Two came covering Vice President Dick Cheney during the final days of the 2004 presidential campaign. Cheney spent the last weekend zigzagging through eight mostly Midwestern and Western battleground states — three of them twice — as he made last-minute pitches for votes. After starting Sunday in Toledo, Ohio, and finishing late Monday at his home in Jackson, Wyo., the Cheney entourage, me included, flew 8,270 miles and spent 22 1/2 of the campaign's final 36 hours on his plane.

Late that Sunday, we flew to Hawaii, which last voted Republican in a presidential election in 1984, in hope of snaring its four electoral votes. Democrat Gore carried the state by 18 percentage points in 2000. But in the 2004 campaign's closing days, polls showed the race between President Bush and Massachusetts Democratic Sen. John Kerry too close to call. Cheney made the exhausting trip in hope of pulling an upset. After all, the national race looked close and every electoral vote counted. So after a Sunday evening campaign stop in Albuquerque, Air Force Two took off for Hawaii, a seven-hour flight. We arrived in Honolulu at 11:30 p.m. local time, motorcaded downtown to the convention center for a midnight rally, quickly filed our stories and motorcaded back to the airport. Following two hours on the ground, we were airborne by 1:30 a.m. local time and flew all night another seven hours back to Colorado, Springs, Colo., where it was snowing on Monday morning. I wrote in the election-eve, Monday Nov, 1 edition of USA TODAY:

"The mood aboard Air Force Two was light Sunday as it shuttled from Ohio to Michigan, Michigan to Iowa and Iowa to New Mexico. Three Cheney granddaughters, Kate Perry, 10, and her sisters Elizabeth, 7, and Grace, 4, played trick-or-treat in the aisles. They wore their costumes onto the stage at a rally in Romulus, Mich. — Kate as a medieval peasant, Elizabeth as the Grim Reaper and Grace as Sleeping Beauty. Cheney's wife, Lynne, introduced their grandchildren. She said Elizabeth, in a skull mask, was 'John Kerry's health plan.'......Cheney, not known as a funnyman, got his biggest laughs with a line he uses to accuse Kerry of talking tough on terrorism after voting in the Senate against major weapons systems. "In Wyoming we have a saying: 'You can put all the lipstick you want on a pig, but at the end of the day, it's still a pig.'"

Despite the grueling 16-hour round trip and a spirited rally in Honolulu, the Bush-Cheney ticket lost Hawaii. But it won the election. Had it lost, Republicans might still be second-guessing the wisdom of that diversion.

But perhaps the pluckiest presidential traveler I ever flew with is former first lady and now New York Democratic Sen. Hillary Rodham Clinton. In the spring of 1999, after attending a memorial service in honor of the students and teachers killed in the Columbine High School shootings, the first lady went off on a Save America's Treasures tour that took her to Santa Fe, Albuquerque and Acoma, N.M. and Mesa Verde, Colo. During that trip, she showed a stamina and an ability to relax rarely seen in top-level politicians.

To get to Mesa Verde, home of the famed cliff dwellings carved into canyon walls more than 700 years ago by the ancestral Pueblo people, Clinton had to fly in a noisy, propeller-driven Air Force cargo plane used to ferry paratroopers over a landing zone. Webbed seats like children's swings hung from the ceiling and earplugs were distributed to passengers to help drown out the jarring vibration from the metal-walled plane's four roaring engines. Even with the earplugs, the noise was overwhelming. But Clinton, after a long morning of climbing up and down ladders and walking in and out of dusty chambers in the cliff dwellings, boarded the military plane, settled herself into one of the suspended web seats, put in her earplugs and promptly fell asleep. While the rest of us bounced, jounced and groused our way back to Albuquerque, teeth chattering all the way,

Hillary slept like a baby. She then resumed her nap on her regular plane, a much more luxurious Air Force Two-type 757, on the way back to Washington.

But an hour or two into the flight, she came back to the press section - barefoot, blond hair askew, without makeup and wrapped in a wool blanket - and proceeded to pick my brain about upstate New York politics. She was at the time contemplating a 2000 run for the New York Senate seat about to be vacated by Daniel P. Moynihan. And knowing I had covered New York politics, she went to work grilling me. To be sure, the most successful politicians never stop working, no matter where they are. And regardless of what they might think of her otherwise, few would dispute the notion that Hillary Rodham Clinton is a hard-working formidable politician.

Clinton is expected to be a 2008 presidential candidate. That campaign, like all campaigns, will put forth a whole new crop of politicians who are people, too. Bring them on. And remember, "You don't boo the president of the United States. If my grandfather ever knew I covered the White House, he would have been very proud.

REFERENCES

Walsh, Kenneth T. 2004. "Air Force One: A History of the Presidents and Their Planes," New York, Hyperion.

About the Author

Richard Benedetto has reported on government and politics on the local, state and national levels for the past 35 years. A native of Utica, N.Y.,Benedetto began his newspaper career with the *Buffalo, (N.Y.) Evening News,* and held government reporting positions with the *Daily Press* and *Observer-Dispatch* in Utica, N.Y. He also worked in the State Capitol bureau of *Gannett News Service* in Albany, N.Y. He is a founding

member of USA TODAY, joining the newspaper in Washington, D.C. in 1982, prior to its debut. USA TODAY is now the nation's largest newspaper.

As a USA TODAY White House/political correspondent, Benedetto has covered the administrations of Ronald Reagan, George H.W. Bush, Bill Clinton and George W. Bush. He has reported on every presidential campaign since 1984. His weekly political column is distributed by the *Gannett News Service* and appears on the USA TODAY website.

Benedetto received his B.A. from Utica College of Syracuse University and holds an M.A. in Journalism from Syracuse University's Newhouse School of Public Communication. Syracuse University awarded him an honorary doctorate in 1992. He has lectured at colleges and universities across the country.

The recipient of numerous journalism awards, he received the 1998 National Italian American Foundation Media Award for his projection of a positive image for Italian-Americans.

xx